D0476584

WITHDRAWN

Best Easy Day Hikes
Houston

Help Us Keep This Guide Up to Date

Every effort has been made by the author and editors to make this guide as accurate and useful as possible. However, many things can change after a guide is published—trails are rerouted, regulations change, facilities come under new management, etc.

We would love to hear from you concerning your experiences with this guide and how you feel it could be improved and kept up to date. While we may not be able to respond to all comments and suggestions, we'll take them to heart and we'll also make certain to share them with the author. Please send your comments and suggestions to the following address:

> Globe Pequot Press
> Reader Response/Editorial Department
> P.O. Box 480
> Guilford, CT 06437

Or you may e-mail us at:

> editorial@GlobePequot.com

Thanks for your input, and happy trails!

Best Easy Day Hikes Series

Best Easy Day Hikes
Houston

Keith Stelter

FALCON GUIDES

GUILFORD, CONNECTICUT
HELENA, MONTANA

AN IMPRINT OF GLOBE PEQUOT PRESS

FALCONGUIDES®

TOPO! Explorer software and SuperQuad source maps courtesy of National
Geographic Maps. For information about TOPO! Explorer, TOPO!, and Nat Geo
Maps products, go to www.topo.com or www.natgeomaps.com.

Project editor: Jessica Haberman
Layout: Kevin Mak
Maps: Offroute Inc. © Morris Book Publishing, LLC

Library of Congress Cataloging-in-Publication Data
Stelter, Keith.
  Best easy day hikes Houston / Keith Stelter.
      p. cm. — (Falconguides)
  ISBN 978-0-7627-5294-2
  1. Hiking—Texas—Houston Region—Guidebooks. 2. Houston (Tex.)—Guide-
books. I. Title.
  GV199.42.T492H688 2009
  917.64'1411–dc22

                                        2009018276

Printed in the United States of America
10 9 8 7 6 5 4 3 2 1

Contents

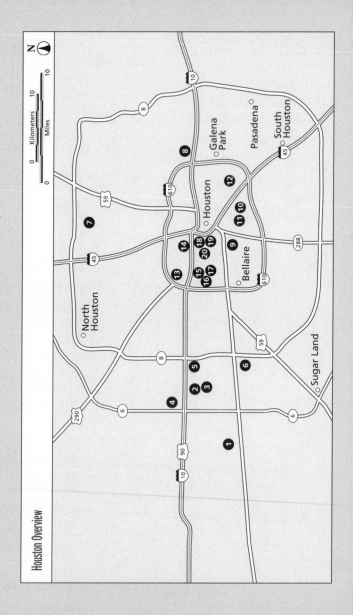

Houston Overview

Acknowledgments

Many people helped make this book possible, and a few went "beyond the call of duty." Thanks to Mark, Scott, and Kay Stelter for their encouragement, ideas, patience, and proofreading. And thanks to Houston Parks superintendent Roy Vasquez for his help on Herman Brown Park and Joe Blanton for his assistance and research on the Houston Arboretum.

Dozens of other people provided information about history, geology, flora and fauna, and hikes they considered "the best easy day hikes." I appreciate their work and thank all of them.

Introduction

The purpose of this guide is to introduce readers to the variety of hiking opportunities in the Houston area. In many hiking guides the hike descriptions are generally point-to-point narratives, getting you safely from the trailhead to the trail's end and back again. However, including information on area flora, fauna, history, and geology adds a great deal of interest to many hikers, including families with young children.

I spent several months researching, talking with park personnel and other folks, hiking and sometimes rehiking trails, and studying the area for interesting facts, scenery, history, and geology. I talked with a variety of hikers, asking them what they wanted a hike description to cover and what made a "best easy day hike." I used the following criteria to select the hikes included in this guide: fun, exercise, family experience, scenery, history, bayous, first-time hiker, experienced hiker, moderate length (1 to 5 miles), dog friendliness, and wheelchair accessibility. Loops and interconnecting loop trails were selected where possible so that a "best" hike within a park could be fashioned by combining the best of several trails.

Determining the best easy day hikes in the Houston area was a combination of personal judgment about what level of hiker the hike was geared for and information from park staff and other hikers. Four of my favorite hikes are the loop trail at the Houston Arboretum, the interconnecting loops in Memorial Park, the Bear Creek Trail, and Herman Brown Park trails. Hiking city and county trails offers a different experience from hiking in state parks and on backcountry trails. Most of the city trails are paved; a few are lighted at night, creating an entirely new hiking experience. There also can be the distraction of the city itself, with its busy streets, buildings, and commerce. Surprisingly, many of the trails are in wooded areas, providing an unexpected degree of solitude.

Whether providing recreational and educational opportunities, encouraging well-being, exploring history and geology, or bringing together people of all ages, hiking has become an important part of many people's lives. I hope that at least some of the hikes in this guide will become your personal favorites and that this book will prove an informative and interesting read as well as an excellent guide to the best easy day hikes in the Houston area.

Hiking in Houston

Bayous are shallow, slow-moving creeks or streams found in low-lying Southern states, and with four major bayous passing through it, Houston is justifiably called "the Bayou City." Buffalo Bayou runs into downtown, Brays Bayou passes near the Texas Medical Center, White Oak Bayou flows through the Heights and near the northwest area, and Sims Bayou lies in the south of Houston. Originally the bayous were used exclusively for flood control, but since the city recognized the opportunity to build trails along the bayous, they have become a bonanza for hikers.

Due to the efforts of Terese "Terry" Hershey, her husband, Jacob, young congressman George Bush, and a dedicated group of supporters, Buffalo Bayou was saved from having its sides lined with concrete in the 1960s and 1970s. Because of this, the bayou contains an incredibly diverse ecosystem that supports dozens of species of flora and fauna, which add a new dimension to your hike.

Buffalo Bayou winds its way through dozens of suburban communities, giving you an opportunity to find a trail near your neighborhood. From West Houston the bayou heads toward downtown. After passing the Barker Reservoir (Hike 1), the bayou runs through Terry Hershey Park (Hikes 2 and 3) to the Houston Arboretum (Hikes 16 and 17), then Memorial Park (Hike 15) and through downtown Houston (Hikes 18, 19, and 20). White Oak and Buffalo Bayous join in downtown Houston at an area known as Allen's Landing. This is the point where the Allen brothers landed in 1836 and founded Houston.

Hiking in Houston is more than walking along bayous, though. Trails can be found in woods, forests, nature sanctuaries, along community streets, downtown, or a 1-square-block oasis in the middle of a residential community. Some trails are busy with hikers, joggers, and cyclists; others are secluded and far from downtown. The opportunity to vary the scenery you pass on a hike is almost unlimited.

The Central and Coastal Flyways pass over or near the city. This affords a year-round opportunity to enjoy an array of native and migratory birds that use the bayous for shelter and food. Birds to look for throughout the year include ospreys, cardinals, herons, hawks, and egrets.

More than 300 of the 600 bird species recorded in the state have been seen in this region. The best indication of birds being present is hearing their songs. The bluebird sings "chur-lee chur chur-lee," the eastern phoebe repeats "fee-bee fee-bee" from the tops of branches, and the tufted titmouse makes a loud whistlelike "peter peter peter."

Some of the area's most colorful birds include the red-breasted nuthatch, eastern bluebird, yellow-throated warbler, dickcissel, pileated woodpecker, American goldfinch, vermilion flycatcher, hooded merganser, and numerous ducks.

Most mammals are active during the night, so seeing them can be difficult. Look for their tracks around the trail and near streams or bayous. White-tailed deer, nine-banded armadillos (the state small mammal), coyotes, opossums, foxes, raccoons, skunks, and fox squirrels make their homes here. Squirrels, white-tailed deer, and armadillos are common in many hiking areas.

In spring and early summer, when wildflowers set the roadsides ablaze with color, driving to a hiking location can be a visual feast. Commonly seen are coreopsis (yellow); firewheels (red); phlox, Mexican hats, daisies, winecups (purple); and yellow primrose. The Texas bluebonnet, the state flower, is at its peak in late March and early April.

The Texas Parks & Wildlife Department has developed a series of nature trails, including the Great Texas Birding Trail–Central Coast and the Heart of Texas Wildlife Trail–East. Maps and location markers at the sites reference areas where wildlife may be seen.

Houston is the largest city in Texas and the fourth largest in the United States, and its land area is also very large. This is an advantage to hikers, since much of the city was built on forested land, marshes, swamp, or prairie. Some of these areas have been set aside as parks, with miles of trails. The trails along the bayous are called "linear" because they follow the bayou.

The Energy Corridor District was recently selected by the National Park Service's Rivers, Trails and Conservation Assistance Program to receive planning assistance for the West Houston Trail System. Through this partnership, the Park Service and Energy Corridor District will continue to develop and improve trails throughout the area.

The Houston Parks & Recreation Department's trail system spans more than 102 miles; the Harris County Precinct Parks Department trails cover more than 80 miles.

Enjoy the experience of hiking in eastern Texas. The great ecological diversity of the territory, along with the flora and fauna, allows you to fashion trips that are much more than just "hikes in the woods."

Houston Weather

The Houston climate is subtropical with high humidity. Mild winds from the south and southeast carry heat from deserts in Mexico and bring rain, sometimes very heavy, from the Gulf of Mexico. The average low temperature (41 degrees Fahrenheit) is in January and the average high (94 degrees) in July and August. The average yearly rainfall is 47.9 inches. The wettest month is June, averaging 5.3 inches, followed closely by May's 5.2 inches. The driest month is February, with 3 inches of rain.

Current weather and forecasts for the Houston area can be obtained by calling the park contact for the hike you are considering.

Except for high temperatures in July and August and possible showers in May, the weather for hiking in the area is great.

Houston Average Monthly Temperatures

Month	High	Low
January	62	41
February	67	44
March	73	51
April	79	58
May	86	66
June	91	72
July	94	74
August	94	73
September	89	68
October	82	59
November	72	50
December	65	43

Precipitation (Rainfall)

Month	Average
January	3.7
February	3.0
March	3.4
April	3.6
May	5.2
June	5.3
July	3.2
August	3.8
September	4.3
October	4.5
November	4.2
December	3.7

Zero Impact and Trail Etiquette

We have a responsibility to protect, no longer just conquer and use, our wild places. Many public hiking locations are at risk, so please do what you can to use them wisely. The following section will help you better understand what it means to take care of parks and wild places while still making the most of your hiking experience.

- **Stay on the trail.** Anyone can take a hike, but hiking safely and with good conservation practices is an art requiring preparation and proper equipment. Always leave an area as good as—or preferably better—than you found it. Key to doing this is staying on the trail. It's true that a trail anywhere leads nowhere new, but purists will just have to get over it. Trails serve an important purpose: They limit impact on natural areas. Straying from a designated trail can cause damage to sensitive areas—damage that may take the area years to recover from, if it can recover at all. Even simple shortcuts can be destructive.

  Many of the hikes described in this guide are on or near areas ecologically important to supporting endangered flora and fauna. So, please, stay on the trail.

- **Leave no weeds.** Noxious weeds tend to overtake other plants, which in turn affects animals and birds that depend on native plants for food. To minimize the spread of noxious weeds, regularly clean your boots and hiking poles of mud and seeds and brush your dog to remove any weed seeds before heading into a new area. Nonnative invasive plants such as yaupon are particularly destructive and can quickly destroy acres of habitat.

- **Keep your dog under control.** Always obey leash laws, and be sure to bury your dog's waste or pack it out in resealable plastic bags.
- **Respect other trail users.** Often you won't be the only one on the trail. With the rise in popularity of multiuse trails, you'll have to learn a new kind of respect, beyond the nod and "hello" approach of the past. First investigate whether you're on a multiuse trail, and then assume the appropriate precautions.

    Mountain bikers can be like stealth airplanes—you may not hear them coming. Be prepared and find out ahead of time whether you share the trail with them. Cyclists should always yield to hikers, but that's little comfort to the hiker who gets overrun. Be aware, and stay to the right.

    More trails are being designed to be, at least in part, wheelchair accessible. Always step to the side to allow folks in wheelchairs time to navigate the terrain. Make them aware if you are going to pass around them.

First Aid

Sunburn

Wear sunscreen or sunblock, protective clothing, and a wide-brimmed hat. If you do get sunburn, protect the affected area from further sun exposure and treat it with aloe vera gel or a treatment of your choice. Remember that your eyes are vulnerable to damaging radiation as well. Sunglasses can help prevent eye damage from the sun.

Blisters

Be prepared to take care of these hike spoilers by carrying moleskin (a lightly padded adhesive) or gauze and tape. An effective way to apply moleskin is to cut out a circle of the material, remove the center—like a doughnut—and place it over the blistered area.

Insect Bites and Stings
You can treat most insect bites and stings by taking an anti-inflammatory pain medication and applying ice to reduce swelling. A cold compress can sometimes ease the itching and discomfort. Don't pinch or scratch the area—you'll only spread the venom.

Ticks
Ticks can carry diseases such as Rocky Mountain spotted fever and Lyme disease. The best defense is, of course, prevention. If you know you're going to be hiking through an area containing ticks, wear long pants and a long-sleeved shirt. At the end of your hike, do a spot check for ticks (and insects in general).

Poison Ivy, Oak, and Sumac
These skin irritants are prevalent on many of the trails in east Texas, sometimes growing into the trail. They come in the form of a bush or a vine and have leaflets in groups of three (poison ivy and oak), five, seven, or nine. Learn how to spot the plants, and especially show young children what to look for. Few things can spoil a hike, or your life the week after, than coming into contact with poison ivy, oak, or sumac. The allergic reaction, in the form of blisters, usually develops about twelve hours after exposure.

The best defense against these irritants is to wear clothing that covers the arms, legs, and torso. If you think you came into contact with these plants, wash with soap and water as soon as possible. If the rash spreads, you may need to see a doctor.

How to Use This Guide

Twenty hikes are detailed in this guide. The overview map at the beginning of this guide shows the location of each hike by hike number, keyed to the table of contents.

Each hike is accompanied by a route map that shows all the accessible roads and trails, points of interest, access to water, towns, landmarks, and geographical features. It also distinguishes trails from roads, and paved roads from unpaved roads. The selected route is highlighted, and directional arrows point the way.

To aid in quick decision-making, each hike description begins with a short summary to give you a taste of the hiking adventure to follow. You'll learn about the trail terrain and what surprises the route has to offer.

Next you'll find the quick, nitty-gritty details of the hike: hike distance and type (loop, lollipop, or out and back); approximate hiking time; difficulty rating; type of trail surface; best season for the hike; other trail users; canine compatibility; fees and permits; park schedule; map resources, trail contacts, and additional information that will help you on your trek.

Finding the trailhead provides directions from Houston right down to where you'll want to park your car.

The Hike is the meat of the chapter. Detailed and honest, it's a carefully researched impression of the trail. While it's impossible to cover everything, you can rest assured that you won't miss what's important.

Miles and Directions provides mileage cues that identify all turns and trail name changes, as well as points of interest.

Don't feel restricted to the routes and trails mapped in this guide. Stick to marked trails, but be adventurous and use the book as a platform to discover new routes for yourself. One of the simplest ways to begin is to turn the map upside down and hike the trail in reverse. The change in perspective can make the hike feel quite different; it's like getting two hikes for one.

You may wish to copy the directions for the course onto a small sheet to help you while hiking, or photocopy the map and cue sheet to take with you. Otherwise, just slip the whole book in your pocket and take it with you. Enjoy your time in the outdoors—and remember to pack out what you pack in.

Map Legend

═🔟═	Interstate Highway
═90═	U.S. Highway
═6═	State Highway
═══	Local/Forest Road
= = = =	Unimproved Road
├──┼──┤	Railroad
- - - - -	Trail
▬▬▬▬	Featured Route
▬▬▬	Paved Trail
	Local/State Park Fill
	Marsh/Swamp
───────	Small River or Creek
⬭	Lake or Pond
‿	Bridge
╎	Gate
❷	Information
🅿	Parking
■	Point of Interest
🚻	Restroom
‖‖‖‖‖	Steps/Boardwalk
○	Town
❻	Trailhead
🗺	Viewpoint

Trail Finder

Best Hikes for Families and Children

Best Hikes for Bayou/Stream Lovers

Best Hikes for History Lovers

Best Hikes for Nature Lovers and Bird-Watchers

Best Hikes for Dogs

Best Hikes for the Physically Challenged

Best Hikes for Runners

Best Hikes for Sun Lovers

Best Hikes for Forest Lovers

Best Hikes for Urban Setting Lovers

1 George Bush Park: Barker to Bayou Bridge

This trail is located in 7,800-acre George Bush Park, part of the 13,500-acre Barker Reservoir. It is the largest park in Harris County and the sixth-largest city park in the nation. This area was part of the original Stephen F. Austin Colony. Wildlife, including shorebirds, can be seen around the bridge over the bayou.

Distance: 2.1 miles out and back

Approximate hiking time: 1 hour

Difficulty: Easy; flat paved surface with no elevation gain

Trail surface: Asphalt

Best season: September to June

Other trail users: Cyclists, in-line skaters, dog walkers

Canine compatibility: Leashed dogs permitted

Fees and permits: No fees or permits required

Schedule: 7:00 a.m. to 10:00 p.m.

Maps: USGS Clodine and Addicks; large map board showing trails and mileages located in the sports complex area

Trail contacts: Harris County Precinct 3 Parks, 3535 War Memorial Dr., Houston 77084; (281) 496-2177

In addition: There are no restrooms or potable water at the trailhead. Located completely inside Barker Reservoir, this trail is sometimes flooded. Call the park at (281) 531-1592 to check conditions.

Finding the trailhead: From the intersection of TX 6 South and I-10 West, continue south on TX 6 for 3.4 miles. Turn right onto FM 1093 (Westheimer Road); go 2.6 miles to 16756 Westheimer Rd. (George Bush Park) and turn right at the park entrance. Follow the entrance road to Beeler and South Cypress Roads. Turn left into the Equestrian and Hike and Bike parking lot. The trail is 20 miles west

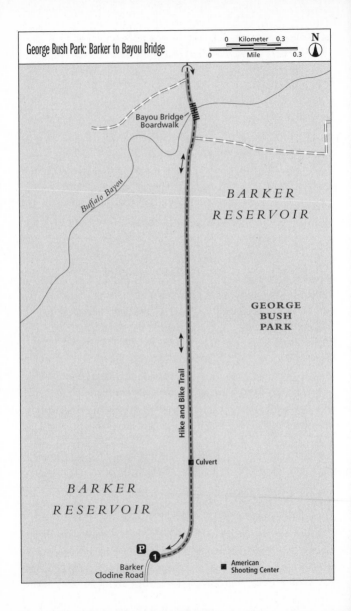

George Bush Park: Barker to Bayou Bridge

0   Kilometer   0.3

0   Mile   0.3

N

Bayou Bridge Boardwalk

Buffalo Bayou

BARKER RESERVOIR

GEORGE BUSH PARK

Hike and Bike Trail

Culvert

BARKER RESERVOIR

P

1

Barker Clodine Road

American Shooting Center

of downtown Houston. *DeLorme: Texas Atlas & Gazetteer:* Page 128
I1. GPS: N29 44.154' / W95 41.138'

The Hike

Start at the trailhead at the entrance gate on the north side
of the parking lot. The trail is asphalt, 10 feet wide, and
wheelchair and stroller accessible. This trail has little canopy
cover, so be sure to take water, a hat, and sunscreen. The
closest potable water is at the sports center, about 2 miles
north. The American Shooting Center is adjacent to the
trail, on the right (east) side. The center is shielded by a
fence and woods, but on weekend a few "pop-pops" from
the trapshooters can be heard.

Follow the trail straight (north) from the trailhead. Both
sides of the trail are mowed grass, with few trees until the
edge of the woods. This is a multiuse trail, so keep to the
right and be wary of cyclists. Stay on the trail and do not
attempt to explore the woods—copperheads and water
moccasins, both venomous snakes, call the bayou home.

Pass a clearing on the left with a wide mowed path heading west toward Buffalo Bayou that is used by park maintenance personnel. Both sides of the trail are mowed for
about 40 feet to the edge of the woods. After heavy rains,
the sides of the trail can be swampy. The hardwood trees get
larger, and a few ferns can be seen at the edge of the woods.
Depending on the season, butterflies flit across the trail and
a variety of birds can be heard in the woods.

Bend slightly right (east) and reach the large wooden
bridge over the bayou. Famous in its own right, the bridge
is known locally as "the Boardwalk." It is about 0.25 mile
long and includes observation platforms and opportunities
for photo ops. The bayou meanders lazily from the left

(west) about 4 feet below the bridge. Heavy woods, water plants, and ferns fill the swampy area. Large turtles, white egrets, great blue herons, and a variety of warblers may be seen at various times of year.

The boardwalk is the high point of the hike, so take time to enjoy it. Cross the bridge and continue, bearing slightly left toward the bayou. Follow the trail north as it runs parallel to the bayou for about 300 feet. This is a good point to turn around and backtrack to the trailhead. For the more energetic, the park contains more than 12 miles of trails to explore.

Miles and Directions

0.0   Start at the trailhead located on the north side of the parking lot. Head north on the asphalt trail.

0.2   Follow trail straight ahead, then bear left (northwest) and shortly bear right (north).

0.3   Pass over a culvert that drains water from the left (west) side of the trail to the right (east) side.

0.4   Still following the asphalt trail, bear slightly left (northwest) and then head straight (north).

0.6   Pass a mowed clearing on the left (west) that leads to a mowed pathway used by maintenance vehicles. Continue straight ahead.

0.9   Bearing slightly right, follow the trail and reach a wooden bridge over Buffalo Bayou.

1.0   Reach the end of the wooden bridge and continue a short distance on the trail. As you pass over a culvert, there is a clearing on the left (west) leading to the bayou. The trail parallels the bayou channel, about 60 feet to the left. The trail continues to the sports complex.

1.05   Turn around and backtrack to the trailhead.

2.1   Arrive back at the trailhead and parking lot.

2 Terry Hershey Park: Cardinal and Blue Jay Loop Trails

This hike is for nature enthusiasts and dog walkers, with dog drinking fountains located along the trail. Depending on the season, wildflowers and blooming shrubs line the sides of the bayou and many species of trees and birds can be seen. Be sure to visit the walk-in sundial, where the shadow you cast shows the time. This lighted path can be enjoyed in the evening.

Distance: 2.3-mile loop

Approximate hiking time: 1.5 hours

Difficulty: Easy; flat terrain and paved path

Trail surface: Asphalt, concrete

Best season: Year-round

Other trail users: Cyclists, in-line skaters, dog walkers

Canine compatibility: Leashed dogs permitted

Fees and permits: No fees or permits required

Schedule: 7:00 a.m. to 10:00 p.m.

Maps: USGS Hedwig Village and Addicks; map trail boards in park; park map available at www .pct3.hctx.net/parks/terryhershey .aspx

Trail contacts: Harris County Precinct 3 Parks, 3535 War Memorial Dr., Houston 77084; (281) 496-2177

In addition: The trail is lighted for evening hiking.

Finding the trailhead: From the junction of I-10 West and US 90, go 15.8 miles west on US 90. Take exit 753A and drive 0.7 mile to Eldridge Parkway. Turn right onto Memorial Drive. Turn right after 0.3 mile into Terry Hershey Park at 15200 Memorial Dr. *DeLorme: Texas Atlas & Gazetteer:* Page 128 I3. GPS: N29 46.862' / W95 37.467'

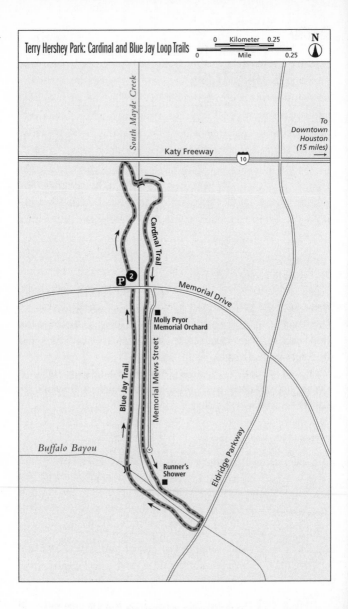

0   Kilometer   0.25

0   Mile   0.25

N

South Mayde Creek

To Downtown Houston (15 miles)

Katy Freeway

10

Cardinal Trail

P 2

Memorial Drive

Molly Pryor Memorial Orchard

Memorial Mews Street

Blue Jay Trail

Buffalo Bayou

Runner's Shower

Eldridge Parkway

The Hike

Start the Cardinal Trail at the trailhead on the north side of the parking lot. There is a large map on a mounted board by the fence just before the park entrance. Near the gate are restrooms and a water fountain. The trail is paved and wheelchair accessible. There is scant tree canopy on the trail to give shade, so be sure to protect yourself with sunscreen and a hat.

Take the connector path by the gazebo to reach the analemmatic sundial—an interesting spot to spend a few minutes. Stand on the month of the year etched in concrete; if the sun is shining, your shadow will be cast across the time of day. Returning to the trail, turn right and head north.

Reach a low stone wall and follow the left leg of the loop, heading north toward I-10. Complete the loop, returning to the starting point. Take the trail left (east) and cross two bridges over South Mayde Creek. There are apartment buildings on the left. Follow the trail as it uses the underpass for Memorial Drive. This section of the hike goes through the park playground and picnic area.

Cardinal Trail ends and the Blue Jay Trail starts. Memorial Mews Street is on the left. An exit from the trail leads to the Molly Pryor Memorial Orchard—an interesting twenty-minute side trip. The creek continually running alongside the trail adds interest to the hike. Pass some exercise stations and a "runner's shower." At this point, South Mayde Creek flows into Buffalo Bayou. Bearing southeast, reach the Eldridge Street bridge and cross over the bayou. Going under the bridge to the southeast side leads to Quail Trail, an out-and-back hike of several miles.

Turn right at the end of the bridge and follow the trail along Buffalo Bayou. The right edge of the trail slopes down to the bayou. The edges are tree and bush covered, ideal habitat for birds. There are a few up-and-down slopes and squiggles to the right and left as the trail heads northwest. Benches are placed strategically along the trail's edge if you need a rest.

Reach a footbridge on the right (northeast); cross over Buffalo Bayou and continue following Blue Jay Trail along South Mayde Creek. Depending on the season, this section can have numerous birds, including robins, cardinals, wrens, and butterflies. Numerous loblolly pines are scattered along the trail's edge. Some earth mounds have been built on the left of the trail to help hide commercial development. Follow the trail north and under Memorial Drive to arrive back at the parking area.

Miles and Directions

0.0 Start at the Cardinal Trail trailhead, just north of the parking lot.

0.1 Reach the analemmatic sundial. Stand on the appropriate stone for the month of the year to show the time with your shadow.

0.4 Reach a rock-paved resting area with a low wall where the path splits. Take the left (west) path toward I-10.

0.5 Follow the path as it makes a broad turn just ahead of I-10 and return to the rock-paved resting area. Turn left (east) and cross two bridges over South Mayde Creek. Then make a hard right, following the path south.

0.8 Use the underpass under Memorial Drive, where Cardinal Trail ends and Blue Jay Trail starts.

0.9 Pass a portable toilet on the left (east), a few benches, and some picnic tables with fire grills. South Mayde Creek is on the right (west).

1.1 Pass an entry gate about 35 feet to the left (east) that leads to Memorial Mews Street and Molly Pryor Memorial Orchard. Continue straight (south) on the paved trail.

1.4 Pass the runner's shower and water fountain on the left (east) and follow the trail, which makes a hard left turn (southeast).

1.5 Pass a bench, where the trail immediately branches. Take the right branch toward Eldridge Parkway. (FYI: The left branch joins the Quail Trail.) A large signboard with a map of the park shows the trails.

1.7 Come to Eldridge Parkway; turn right (southwest) and take the pedestrian walkway on the bridge over Buffalo Bayou. Continue straight and meet the trail on the other side.

1.8 Reach a wooden bridge on the right and cross South Mayde Creek, heading east. Then follow the trail north.

2.2 A sign on the left (southwest) displays the park rules. At the Y junction bear right (northwest). In about 100 feet go under Memorial Parkway and follow the trail to parking lot.

2.3 Arrive back at the parking lot.

3 Terry Hershey Park: Robin and Robin Loop Trails

This hike is for those who enjoy a hike with a change of pace. The trail presents two faces. The first section traverses up and down gentle slopes with woods and follows Buffalo Bayou. The second section is an easy loop that follows a concrete drainage canal, surrounded by a few trees and residences. Each section of the trail has its own name. The section following the bayou is Robin Trail; the other is Robin Loop.

Distance: 2.2-mile lollipop
Approximate hiking time: 1.5 hours
Difficulty: Easy; relatively flat, mostly paved trail
Trail surface: Asphalt, concrete, crushed granite
Best season: Year-round
Other trail users: Cyclists, in-line skaters, dog walkers
Canine compatibility: Leashed dogs permitted
Fees and permits: No fees or permits required
Schedule: 7:00 a.m. to 10:00 p.m.
Maps: USGS Clodine and Addicks; park map available at www.pct3.hctx.net/parks.
Trail contacts: Harris County Precinct 3 Parks, 3535 War Memorial Dr., Houston; (281) 496-2177
In addition: There are no restroom facilities available on this hike.

Finding the trailhead: From the junction of I-10 West and US 90, go 15.1 miles west on US 90. Take exit 753B and drive 0.3 mile to Dairy Ashford Street. Turn left onto South Dairy Ashford Street and drive 0.5 mile. Turn into the parking lot at 1001 South Dairy Ashford St. The Terry Hershey Park gate and trailhead are located at the end of the parking lot. *DeLorme: Texas Atlas & Gazetteer:* Page 128 J3. GPS: N29 45.692' / W95 43.446'

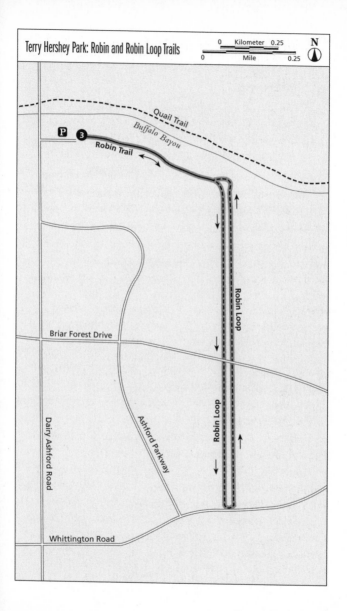

Terry Hershey Park: Robin and Robin Loop Trails

Kilometer
Mile

N

Quail Trail

Buffalo Bayou

P 3 Robin Trail

Robin Loop

Robin Loop

Briar Forest Drive

Dairy Ashford Road

Ashford Parkway

Whittington Road

The Hike

Start the Robin Trail at the trailhead just inside the park gate. There is a large map of the park mounted next to the gate. The paved trail is wheelchair accessible, but several steep slopes may make using a wheelchair impractical. This underutilized trail provides a great hike for those wanting a little solitude.

Head east down a slope, passing an earth mound on the left and then crossing a bridge over large culverts. The mix of hardwood trees includes bur oak, live oak, sycamore, willow, dogwood, and yaupon, a very invasive small tree. These hardwoods plus a few loblolly pines furnish good habitat for animals and birds. The trees provide a good canopy, making the hike more enjoyable. Benches are placed conveniently along the trail, some of them facing the bayou.

Buffalo Bayou can be seen on the left (north) about 50 feet away. Sometimes the left edge of the trail drops sharply to the bayou, so use caution. Reach a bridge with a small stream flowing under it. These unnamed creeks are called "meanders." That's the local term for segments of Buffalo Bayou that have been left behind as the bayou changed course over the years.

Following the trail east; turn right at the T and head due south. This is the beginning of the Robin Loop. The bayou continues east, away from the loop. This section of the hike is unusual because the entire loop is in your line of sight. The long, narrow loop has a row of trees on each side, and a fence partially shields residences on the east and west sides.

The loop goes south to Whittington Road and then turns north. A concrete-sided drainage canal in the center runs the length of the loop. Mowed grass and a few plantings including crepe myrtle cover the ground around the loop. The interior sides of the trail slope sharply down about 25 feet to the canal, so watch your step. Complete the loop at the T intersection where it started. Turn right and backtrack to the trailhead.

The park is named in honor of Terry Hershey, who with her husband and friends, including young congressman George Bush, worked together to have 500 acres set aside for a park. They also convinced the authorities not to pave the sides of Buffalo Bayou, as had been the practice at the time.

Miles and Directions

0.0   Start at the trailhead at the gate on the east side of the parking area. Follow the trail down a slope and over a bridge.

0.1   Continue following the asphalt trail with a slight bend right (east)

0.3   After going down a minor slope, reach a bridge that crosses a stream that joins the bayou. Then continue following the trail.

0.4   The asphalt trail changes to a surface of small packed granite. Follow the trail, which curves slightly right.

0.5   Reach a T and turn right, heading south to begin the Robin Loop.

0.6   Pass residences within 10 feet of the right trail edge, and then pass a concrete flood-control structure down a slope on the left.

0.8   Cross over a small metal culvert. Residences are still in view just past a fence on the right.

1.0   Following the trail north, pass through the park gate and then come to a T at Whittington Road. Turn left (east), following along Whittington. Take a hard left, heading north, as

Robin Loop meets the sidewalk. Use caution—this is a busy street.

1.4 Continue following the trail due north and pass a concrete flood-control structure down a slope on the left.

1.6 Reach the end of the loop at the T. Turn right (west) and backtrack to the trailhead.

2.2 Arrive back at the trailhead and return to the parking area.

4 Bear Creek Nature Trail

Hike over an area that had been farmed by German immigrants and their descendants for one hundred years. Deer are common, as are frogs and empty snail shells. Late spring through early fall, venomous snakes (water moccasins and copperheads) as well as several species of nonvenomous snakes may be seen. This pleasant trail traverses a forest of hardwood trees. Enjoy trekking through the woods and exploring nature.

Distance: 3.6-mile loop
Approximate hiking time: 2 hours
Difficulty: Easy; flat forested trail
Trail surface: Bark mulch, dirt
Best season: Year-round
Other trail users: Equestrians for a short distance
Canine compatibility: Dogs not permitted

Fees and permits: No fees or permits required
Schedule: 7:00 a.m. to dusk
Maps: USGS Addicks; park map available at www.pct3.hctx.net/park
Trail contacts: Harris County Precinct 3 Parks, 3535 War Memorial Dr., Houston 77084; (281) 496-2177

Finding the trailhead: From the junction of I-10 West and US 90, go 15.8 miles west on US 90. Take exit 753A toward Eldridge Parkway. Turn right onto North Eldridge Parkway and drive 2.8 miles. Turn left onto War Memorial Drive, and in 0.2 mile turn into Bear Creek Park at 3535 War Memorial Dr. The trailhead and parking are located at the Equestrian Trail parking area. *DeLorme: Texas Atlas & Gazetteer:* Page 128 E2. GPS: N29 49.391' / W95 38.044'

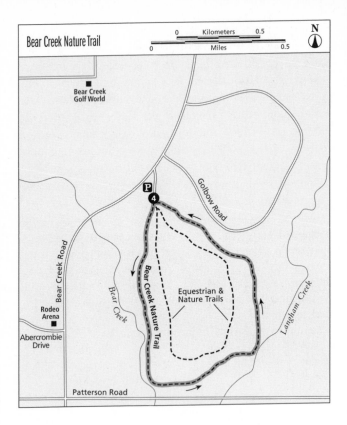

Bear Creek Nature Trail

Kilometers
0   0.5
Miles
0   0.5

N

Bear Creek
Golf World

Golbow Road

Bear Creek Road

Bear Creek

Bear Creek Nature Trail

Equestrian &
Nature Trails

Langham Creek

Rodeo
Arena

Abercrombie
Drive

Patterson Road

The Hike

Start at the trailhead located through a meadow, about
500 feet south of the Equestrian Trail parking area. Turn
right (east) and immediately enter heavy woods. This loop
includes portions of the Nature and Equestrian Trails, so at
times you may be sharing the trail with horses. The trail has
little to no signage, so keep track of your location.

Bear right and then follow the trail straight. Heavy woods, including large oaks, maples, and cedar elms, line the trail. Some of the trees are hung with long strands of Spanish moss.

Many trees in the woods were downed by Hurricane Ike in September 2008. They will be left to decay naturally and furnish nutrients to the forest. One of the uprooted trees along the trail's edge is a water oak. Ironically, the trail-edge sign identifying the fallen tree is still standing. There are no benches along the trail, but it's easy to find a log to rest on.

The trail makes a number of turns to the right and left. Just ahead of a Y, pass a sign on the right stating NATURE TRAIL. Take the left branch, heading east.

Pass through a swampy area where deer tracks are numerous. Try to guess the size of the deer by the size of the track. There are clumps of maidenhair ferns, some 6 feet tall. The trail through the woods gives a constantly changing picture as the seasons change. Any season is a good time to hear birds singing in the woods. Cardinals are easy to spot due to their red feathers.

The trail meanders left and right and sometimes makes a semicircle. While in the swampy area, watch and listen for toads and frogs. Large, empty snail shells are scattered about. Continue following the loop back to the trailhead.

Bear Creek Pioneers Park is located on the Addicks Reservoir, created in the 1940s by the U.S. Army Corps of Engineers to help prevent a recurrence of the catastrophic flooding that happened in Houston in 1935. Bear Creek flows through the park and is one of the major tributaries of Buffalo Bayou. This area is a fertile hiking region, with George Bush Park, Edith Moore Sanctuary, Terry Hershey

Park, Westside Hike and Bike Trail, and Boone Road Park all close by.

Miles and Directions

NOTE: GPS coordinates have been provided for some milepoints. The trail goes through dense woods with no signage and some sections have been blocked by trees downed by Hurricane Ike in September 2008.

0.0 Start at the trailhead on the right at the south end of the parking lot and turn right onto the trail.

0.1 Follow the trail east and immediately go into the woods.

0.2 Follow the trail, bearing left and then right, heading south. Pass clumps of ferns and a NATURE TRAIL sign on the right.

0.3 Reach a Y; take the left branch, which leads through a clearing.

0.5 Follow the trail through a series of left and right meanderings. Reach an uprooted tree on the right, marked by a sign that says WATER OAK (GPS: N29 49.178' / W95 38.135'). Bear left (southeast) at the sign and follow the trail past ferns on the right and left.

0.6 Pass a CEDAR ELM sign on the right (GPS: N29 49.178' / W95 38.135'). Bear left at the sign; continue in an arc to the left (east), and then follow the trail south.

0.7 Follow the trail as it zigzags left, straight, and right.

0.9 Cross over a drain tile running across and under the trail.

1.0 Bear slightly right (southwest) through a swampy area. The trail continues to bend left and right.

1.2 Reach a NATURE TRAIL sign on the right (GPS: N29 48.875' / W95 38.058').

1.3 Pass very large loblolly pine (over 3 feet in diameter and 80 feet tall) at trail's edge on the right.

1.5 Go through a swampy area (depending on when it last rained) bearing left (east) and then following the trail in semicircle to the left (north).

1.6 Follow the trail and bear hard right (east) (GPS: N29 48.902' / W95 37.887').

1.9 Follow the trail, making a hard left (northeast) and then the immediate right (east).

2.1 Follow the trail past some very large trees that were uprooted by Hurricane Ike. The trail continues to meander left and right.

2.6 Continue straight on the trail and then take a hard right (north) (GPS: N29 49.148' / W95 37.575').

2.8 The trail bears left (west) and then follows a short semicircle route.

3.1 The trail zigzags and goes straight. Make a hard right (north) and then proceed west (GPS: N29 49.277' / W95 37.840').

3.5 Reach a Y; take the left (north) branch and then bend to the right. Pass a sign on the left, tacked about 7 feet high in a tree, that says START TALL PINE TRAIL (GPS: N29 49.356' / W98 38.046'). Head into the meadow on the right and walk about 50 yards.

3.6 Arrive back at the trailhead.

5 Edith L. Moore Nature Sanctuary

These short trails are a paradise for bird-watchers and nature lovers. Over 150 species of birds have been seen. This is a great park for families. Within the park's 17.5 acres, cross Rummel Creek and see two oxbows created by the meandering creek. Many bridges and wooden boardwalks add to the hike's interest.

Distance: 1.5 miles of interconnecting loops

Approximate hiking time: 1 hour

Difficulty: Easy; flat, shaded terrain

Trail surface: Mulch and wooden boardwalks

Best season: Year-round

Other trail users: Bird-watchers

Canine compatibility: Dogs not permitted

Fees and permits: No fees or permits required; donations accepted

Schedule: 7:00 a.m. to 7:00 p.m. October 1 through March 31; 7:00 a.m. to 9:00 p.m. April 1 through September 30. Park gates are locked at closing.

Maps: USGS Hedwig Village; park maps available at office

Trail contacts: Houston Audubon Society, 440 Wilchester Blvd., Houston 77079; (713) 932-1639

In addition: Restrooms are available in the Edith L. Moore Cabin.

Finding the trailhead: From the junction of I-10 West and US 90, go 11.7 miles on US 90 to exit 756A toward Beltway 8 (West Sam Houston Parkway). In 0.8 mile turn right onto Memorial Drive. In 0.5 mile turn left onto Wilchester Boulevard. Follow Wilchester to the Edith L. Moore Nature Sanctuary at 440 Wilchester Blvd. and turn left into the parking area. The trailhead is located behind the pioneer cabin adjacent to the parking area. Additional parking is available adjacent to the park in the Memorial United Methodist Church west parking area, located at 12955 Memorial Dr. *DeLorme: Texas Atlas & Gazetteer:* Page 128 I5. GPS: N29 46.286' / W95 34.202'

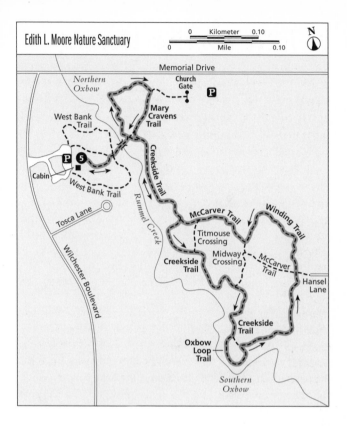

0 Kilometer 0.10
0 Mile 0.10

N

Memorial Drive

Northern
Oxbow

Church
Gate

P

West Bank
Trail

Mary
Cravens
Trail

P 5

Cabin

West Bank Trail

Creekside Trail

Tosca Lane

Rummel Creek

McCarver Trail

Winding Trail

Titmouse
Crossing

Midway
Crossing

McCarver
Trail

Creekside
Trail

Hansel
Lane

Wilchester Boulevard

Creekside
Trail

Oxbow
Loop
Trail

Southern
Oxbow

The Hike

Start the hike behind the Edith L. Moore log cabin. There
are no fewer than ten named trails, combining to create a
hike of 1.5 miles. They loop, interconnect, and join one
another through a series of T and Y intersections. There are
numerous benches placed strategically along the trails. To
add interest to this hike, take along a field guide to birds.

To reach the Creekside Trail, follow a series of board-walks around a small pond, then bear left to the T intersection with the Mary Cravens Trail. Take the right branch of Mary Cravens Trail, heading northeast. Cross Rummel Creek on a wooden bridge. This spot offers good photo ops. Reach the T intersection with Creekside Trail and take the right branch, heading south.

Continue on the trail through the woods and near the creek, listening and watching for birds. Depending on the season, great blue herons and great egrets, both large birds, may be seen along the creek. The woods are alive with the singing of numerous species of birds. The trail heads south over some boardwalks and reaches the junction with McCarver Trail.

Follow the right branch, heading west, which is Creekside Trail. Continue following the trail until nearly reaching Rummel Creek, where the trail makes a hard left and heads south. Listen for the loud drumming of pileated woodpeckers on tree trunks as they look for carpenter ants, a favorite food. This is the largest woodpecker in North America.

Continue south, bearing slightly east and away from the creek; then do a semicircle for a short distance, heading north and then bearing right (south) over boardwalks. The Midway Crossing dead-ends on the left into Creekside Trail. Stay on Creekside Trail until you reach the Oxbow Loop on the right (west). Follow the loop around to see the Southern Oxbow created by Rummel Creek. An oxbow is created when a creek changes directions and leaves behind an isolated section.

Rejoin Creekside Trail and head east and then north. Follow the Creekside Trail north to where it ends and joins Winding Trail. Continue following Winding Trail to where it ends and joins McCarver Trail. Follow McCarver generally west until it intersects Creekside, the longest trail in the sanctuary. Backtrack to the trailhead and log cabin. Unbelievably, all of this happened in less than 1.5 mile.

The sanctuary is maintained by the Houston Audubon Society. Their administrative offices are located on the park grounds.

Miles and Directions

No miles or directions are provided for this hike. The park has numerous short interconnecting trails on 17.5 acres.

6 Boone Road Park

This 27-acre park with a short trail is a good hike for families with young children. The entire trail is paved and flat, circling a center area that contains a small playground, picnic tables, a shelter, and a cricket field. It is one of the few parks in Houston where cricket matches can be viewed. Brays Bayou runs along one edge, affording a chance to see birds.

Distance: 1.1-mile loop
Approximate hiking time: 45 minutes
Difficulty: Easy; flat terrain and paved trail
Trail surface: Asphalt
Best season: Year-round
Other trail users: Dog walkers, in-line skaters
Canine compatibility: Leashed dogs permitted

Fees and permits: No fees or permits required
Schedule: 6:00 a.m. to 11:00 p.m.
Maps: USGS Alief; park maps available at www.houstontx.gov/parks/trails.html
Trail contacts: Houston Parks and Recreation Department (HPARD), 2999 S. Wayside Dr., Houston 77023; (713) 865-4500

Finding the trailhead: From the junction of I-10 West and US 90 merge onto US 59 via exit 770A. Follow US 59 south and take the Beechnut Street exit. Turn right onto Beechnut Street and in 2.6 miles turn right onto Wilcrest Drive. Then turn right onto Boone Road and proceed to Boone Road Park at 7700 Boone Rd. Turn right into the paved parking lot. The trailhead is adjacent to the parking area. *DeLorme: Texas Atlas & Gazetteer:* Page 128 I1. GPS: N29 41.701' / W95 34.529'

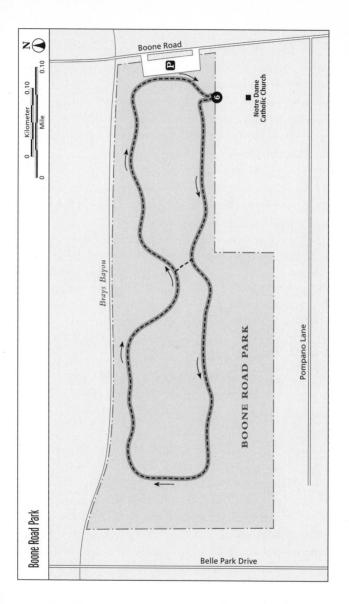

Boone Road Park

The Hike

Start the trail on the left (south) side of the paved loop and head west. The loop rings the park, closely following the park boundaries. This 27-acre park is bordered by Notre Dame Catholic Church on the south, power lines on the west, Brays Bayou and residences on the north, and Boone Road on the east.

The entire trail is wheelchair and stroller accessible. There is no canopy cover, so wear a hat and sunscreen. Inside the loop there's a playground, a shelter, benches, picnic tables, and a cricket field.

There's the possibility of seeing a cricket match, a game with some similarity to baseball. The batters use bats that are oblong with skinny handles. The pitcher is called the "bowler," and runs are scored in a totally different way than in baseball. Trying to figure out what's going on in the cricket match can add interest to the hike.

Head straight west; Notre Dame Catholic Church is on the left and a playground on the right. The trail has a few easy curves right and left but is basically straight. After 0.2 mile come to a Y and follow the left (straight) branch, still heading west. There is a drinking fountain and bench on the left side of the trail.

Continue straight (west), with a few squiggles right and left. Residences can be seen on the left. Pass over a culvert and then make a hard right, heading north. At 0.5 mile make a hard right, heading east. Brays Bayou is on the left, about 30 feet from the trail's edge. Residences can be seen beyond the bayou. It's worth walking to the bayou to possibly see waterbirds or other animals. Be careful at the edge of the bayou; it slopes down sharply.

Bend right and pass a DESIGNATED NATURAL AREA sign about 20 feet on the left. The trail follows along the edge of this reforesting project for 0.25 mile, a great area for viewing birds and other wildlife. Reach a Y junction and take the left (straight leg) branch, heading east. Pass two volleyball/badminton courts on the right. Follow right and then straight (south) and pass a sidewalk on the left leading to the parking lot and Boone Road. The portable toilet on the left is the only toilet facility in the park. End the hike at the parking lot.

Miles and Directions

0.0 Start at the trailhead adjacent to the paved parking area. Take the trail on the left (west) side.

0.2 Follow the asphalt trail, heading straight (west) and reach a Y junction. Take the left branch continuing west.

0.3 The trail bends a little to the left and right; continue straight (west) near the park fence.

0.4 Cross over a culvert and then make a hard right, heading north. Power lines are on the left.

0.5 Continue straight (north) until the trail makes a hard right (east). Follow the trail east, with Brays Bayou and residences on left side and the playground and cricket field on the right.

0.6 Follow the trail east as it wanders a little to the right and left.

0.7 Follow the trail as it bends right (east) and pass a DESIGNATED NATURAL AREA sign on the left (north). The area is partially fenced and is being reforested.

0.8 Continue straight, going east until you reaching a Y junction. Take the left (north) branch. (FYI: The right branch connects to the south side of the loop.)

0.9 Pass a sidewalk on the right (south) that leads to two volleyball/badminton courts on the right. Continue following the trail east.

1.0 Walk straight ahead (east) on the trail, with the playground about 10 feet away on the right (south) and Boone Road on the left (east).

1.1 Arrive back at the trailhead and parking lot on the left.

7 Keith-Weiss Park

It's always great to find a new trail. This trail around the flood-control detention ponds was opened in August 2008. The paved trail takes advantage of both the forest and the ponds. An area was cleared for the ponds in the surrounding forest in this 500-acre park, and the fish and birds have already moved in. A curving boardwalk with observation platforms and benches crosses the main pond, and there are many good photo ops.

Distance: 2.3-mile lollipop

Approximate hiking time: 1.5 hours

Difficulty: Easy; paved trail with little up and down

Trail surface: Concrete sidewalks

Best season: Year-round

Other trail users: Dog walkers, cyclists, bird-watchers

Canine compatibility: Leashed dogs permitted

Fees and permits: No fees or permits required

Schedule: Dawn to dusk

Maps: USGS Humble; park maps available at www.houstontx.gov/parks/trails.html

Trail contacts: Houston Parks and Recreation Department (HPARD), 2999 S. Wayside Dr., Houston 77023; (713) 865-4500

In addition: A portable toilet is located at the parking area. Scooters and skateboards are prohibited.

Finding the trailhead: From I-10 East take exit 768A on the left to merge onto I-45 toward Dallas. Follow I-45 to exit 51 and merge onto I-610 East. Take exit 19B off I-610 East for the Hardy Toll Road North. In 3 miles exit the Hardy Toll Road at the Little York Road exit. Follow Little York Road and turn left onto Aldine Westfield Road. Follow Aldine Westfield for 1.3 miles and turn into Keith-Weiss Park at 12030 Aldine Westfield Rd. The trailhead is located at the end of the

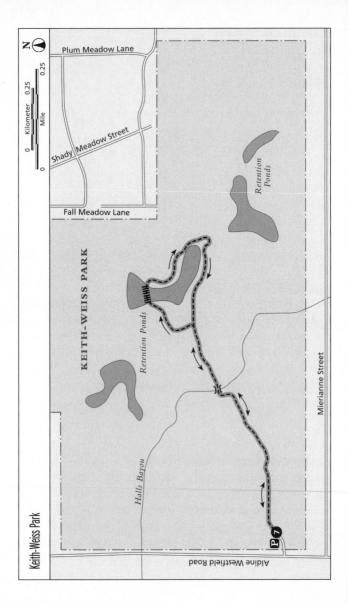

Keith-Weiss Park

parking area. *DeLorme: Texas Atlas & Gazetteer:* Page 130 A3. GPS: N29 53.397' / W95 21.285'

The Hike

Start the trail, which is all on concrete sidewalks with a few minor up-and-down grades, from the northwest side of the parking area. The sidewalks are just inside the park gate. Take the right branch of the trail, heading away from the soccer fields. Two pavilions and a playground are on the left. Follow the trail as it veers left past tennis courts. At about 0.25 mile leave the playground/ball field area and enter the woods. The woods are mostly hardwoods, including live oaks, with a few large loblolly pines. The trail is cleared for about 15 feet to the woods on each side.

The bridge that crosses Halls Bayou provides an opportunity to inspect the bayou, which bisects the park. Shorebirds may be seen along the edges of the bayou. The trail alternates between partial and no tree canopy, so wear a hat and sunscreen.

Birds may be heard in the woods, including the distinct notes of the song sparrow. Listen for three or four notes followed by a "tow-wee." There are some interesting stone blocks along the trail, some of them large enough to sit on.

As you approach the retention ponds, you'll notice that the terrain has been altered by bulldozers. The forest has been cleared and the land shaped to slope down gently to the basins. The landscaping expertly blends the ponds with the surrounding forest. Birds and other water-loving creatures have made the ponds home, and bird watchers are already considering this a premier location.

The hike follows around and across the ponds. A large

wooden boardwalk winds its way over the largest pond. Several observation areas built on the boardwalk have benches and informational signs. Depending on the season, there are hundreds of birds around or in the pond, including egrets, herons, ducks, and a variety of other species. A smaller pond joins the larger pond via an overflow ditch.

Follow the trail going around the pond, which is on the right. Pass a wooden observation deck at the edge of the pond. Continue following the trail going away from the ponds until you reach a Y. There are two large orange rectangular stones at this point. Take the left branch and backtrack to the trailhead.

This 500-acre park in the middle of a forest on the city's northeast side holds great promise to hikers, as more trails are planned.

Miles and Directions

0.0 Start at the trailhead (concrete sidewalk) at the northeast corner of the parking area.

0.2 Reach a T intersection and take the right (east) branch. Pass tennis courts on the right and head into a wooded area.

0.3 Bear right, following trail, and pass an incoming sidewalk on the left (north).

0.4 Follow the trail as it bends left, right, and goes straight.

0.5 Cross over a culvert and then a bridge that crosses Halls Bayou. Cross over another culvert shortly after the end of the bridge.

0.75 Pass some rock slabs on the right and left, large enough to sit on, and reach a T intersection. Take the left (north) branch and continue following the trail.

0.8 Pass a bench on the left and an information sign on the right that tells about helping nature make stormwater cleaner.

0.9 Continue toward the retention ponds and bear slightly left (north). Then head right (east) and reach the boardwalk that crosses the ponds.

1.0 After crossing the pond, curve right and head south. The retention pond is on the right. Follow the trail and bend slightly left (east), following around the pond edge.

1.2 Bear slightly left (east) and pass a stone retaining wall at the end of the pond.

1.3 Follow the trail around the pond and reach a T intersection. Take the right branch and cross an overflow ditch from another pond. The main retaining pond is on the right.

1.4 Go past an observation deck on the right, at the edge of the pond. Continue straight and then bear right going north. The main pond is to the right.

1.6 Pass two large, orange rectangular stones and reach an inverted Y junction. Take the branch to the left (straight) and backtrack to the trailhead.

2.3 Arrive back at the trailhead and return to the parking area.

8 Herman Brown Park

This 750-acre park on the northeast edge of the city is an oasis for hikers. Even though the park is surrounded by residential communities, its trails pass through bottomland hardwood forest containing live oak, black willow, and cypress. Hunting Bayou adds interest as it bisects the park. The bayou also attracts neotropical birds as they stop on their migration flights.

Distance: 2.8 miles of interconnecting loops with a short out-and-back section
Approximate hiking time: 1.5 hours
Difficulty: Easy; paved flat trail
Trail surface: Asphalt, crushed granite, mulch
Best season: Year-round
Other trail users: Dog walkers
Canine compatibility: Leashed dogs permitted

Fees and permits: No fees or permits required
Schedule: 5:00 a.m. to 10:00 p.m.
Maps: USGS Jacinto City; park maps available at www.houston tx.gov/parks/trails.html
Trail contacts: Houston Parks and Recreation Department (HPARD), 2999 S. Wayside Dr., Houston 77023; (713) 845-1000

Finding the trailhead: From the junction of I-10 East and US 59, follow I-10 for 5.6 miles to exit 776A toward Mercury Drive. After 0.1 mile bear slightly left onto East Freeway. In 0.2 mile turn left onto Mercury Drive. Continue straight and turn into Herman Brown Park at 400 Mercury Dr., northeast of the I-10 and I-610 interchange. The trailhead is located at the end of the parking area. *DeLorme: Texas Atlas & Gazetteer:* Page 131 H8. GPS: N29 46.955' / W95 14.739'

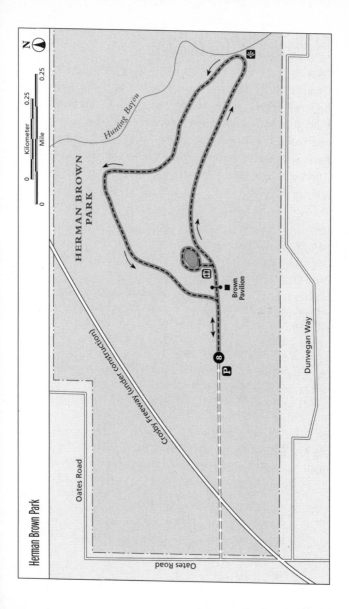

Herman Brown Park

The Hike

Start the hike from the east side of the parking area just past the gate at the asphalt maintenance road. Turn right, heading east. There are lights on the left side, allowing some hiking after dusk. Due to Hurricane Ike in September 2008 and extensive road construction on I-610 that divided the park, the former trail names are no longer applicable.

Pass a few picnic tables on the right and then cross a short wooden bridge over a shallow gully. Reach the Brown Pavilion, where there are water fountains and restrooms. There are two tennis courts on the left, and the area is lighted.

There are stone trail marker posts at the intersection of most trails. They are mainly used to identify points of interest, such as the lake, the bayou overlook, the direction to the Brown Pavilion, and the direction to the soccer/baseball fields.

Turn left onto a gravel trail that leads to a very small lake; the path follows around the lake, which is stocked with rainbow trout during January and February by the Texas Parks & Wildlife Department. It is probably best to avoid the elbow-to-elbow crowds of fishermen during these periods. The area around the lake can be swampy, depending on the amount of rainfall. Backtrack from the lake to the main trail and resume the hike from the turnoff.

Continue following the trail and signs to reach the Hunting Bayou overlook. Pass live oaks, willows, cypress trees, and a few loblolly pines, with a scattering of palmettos as part of the forest understory. In any season of the year, birds can be heard singing in the woods.

A stone marker identifies the wooden platform, which

is situated about 30 feet above the bayou. The bayou forms a lazy S as it flows from north to south. Hunting Bayou is a tributary of Buffalo Bayou, and both are magnets for migrating birds. Great blue herons and white egrets are among the birds commonly seen at the water's edge. Backtrack to the main trail.

Continue following the main trail, which has heavy forest on both edges. The trail turns right and left but generally heads west toward I-610 and then back east toward Brown Pavilion. Cross a small wooden bridge over a shallow creek. Follow the trail back to the junction near the Brown Pavilion and backtrack to the trailhead and parking area.

Miles and Directions

0.0 Start at the trailhead adjacent to the east side of the parking area at the gate barring the asphalt maintenance road. Head straight (east).

0.1 Pass a picnic table and a path on the right (south) that makes a small loop and rejoins this trail.

0.2 Pass a picnic table and path on the left that dead-ends into the trail. Continue straight and cross a short bridge over a gully.

0.25 Pass a gate blocking the trail. The Brown Pavilion is ahead on the right and tennis courts are on the left. There are water fountains and restrooms at the pavilion. Continue straight on a narrow crushed-granite trail.

0.3 Reach a crossing where a trail leads right and left. Turn left, heading north toward a very small lake. Reach the lake, where a loop trail around the lake joins this trail on the left. Take the trail on the left.

0.4 Follow around the lake and return to the point where the lake loop started; return to the main trail.

0.5 Reach a stone trail marker on the left and tennis court on the right. Turn left, heading east on the asphalt trail.

0.6 Continue straight on the trail and then make a hard left heading north at a bench on the right side.

0.8 Reach a T intersection and take the right branch, heading east. There is a bench and stone trail maker.

1.1 Turn left onto an asphalt trail. Head north for 0.1 mile and then make a hard right, heading southeast.

1.25 Reach a trail marker and make a hard left, heading northeast and to the bayou overlook.

1.3 Reach the bayou overlook platform. Hunting Bayou lies below the platform to the northeast. Follow the trail from the overlook, heading northwest.

1.7 Continue following the trail northwest until you reach a bridge. Past the bridge bear slightly to the right, heading north.

1.9 Follow the trail and take a hard left, heading west.

2.2 Take a hard left onto a path, heading south.

2.3 Cross a bridge and follow the trail to the right, heading west.

2.6 Follow the trail, making a hard left turn and heading south. In less than 0.1 mile reach the T intersection with the asphalt maintenance road near the Brown Pavilion. Take the right branch, heading west to the trailhead.

2.8 Arrive back at the trailhead.

9 Hermann Park

This is a great hike for the entire family. Three new islands on the enlarged McGovern Lake supply wetland habitat. There are many amenities for young hikers, including a miniature train ride and the Houston Zoo—advantages a city hike can have over country hikes. Hermann Park is Houston's most developed park and, with more than five million visitors, one of the most visited. Philanthropist George Hermann gave Houston 285 acres for the park in May 1914.

Distance: 1.8-mile loop
Approximate hiking time: 1 hour
Difficulty: Easy; flat paved trails
Trail surface: Crushed packed granite, concrete
Best season: Year-round
Other trail users: Dog walkers, joggers, cyclists, tourists
Canine compatibility: Leashed dogs permitted
Fees and permits: No fees or permits required
Schedule: 6:00 a.m. to 11:00 p.m.
Maps: USGS Bellaire; park maps available at www.hermannpark .org/directions.html
Trail contacts: Houston Parks & Recreation Department (HPARD), 2999 S. Wayside Dr., Houston 77023; (713) 865-4500; www .houstontx.gov/parks/trails.html
In addition: Water fountains are scattered throughout the park. Restroom facilities are located at the Miller Outdoor Theater.

Finding the trailhead: From Memorial Park turn left onto Memorial Drive and then make an easy left onto Woodway Drive. After 0.5 mile turn left onto the West Loop Freeway North. Merge onto I-610 South, and in less than 2 miles merge onto US 59 North at exit 8A toward downtown. Take the Main Street exit and keep straight to go onto Wentworth Street. Follow Wentworth to Fannin Street and turn right. Turn into Hermann Park, north off Fannin Street. *DeLorme: Texas Atlas & Gazetteer:* Page 134 B1. GPS: N29 43.254' / W95 23.506'

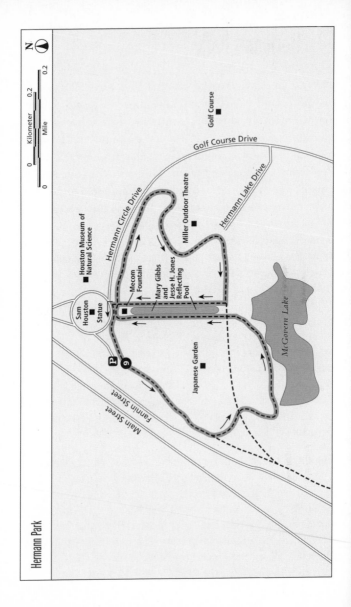

Hermann Park

The Hike

There is no official trailhead for this hike. Use the north entrance parking lot; cross the sidewalk to the wide crushed-gravel trail and turn right. The trail has no signs, but it is virtually impossible to get lost. It is wheelchair and stroller accessible and is lighted for hiking after dusk. The Texas Medical Center is on the southwest edge of the park, so occasionally a helicopter may be heard.

The children's train crosses the trail numerous times, winding its way around the park. This is a "people person" park, and there are always hikers, walkers, joggers, and tourists and generally a busload of schoolchildren. The various park users combine with all the amenities to make this an interesting hike.

Pass near a fenced area on the left, which encloses the Japanese garden. For this short section of the hike, Fannin Street will be on the right. The trail bears generally left or straight ahead. Large live oak trees are scattered along the trail, many with Spanish moss trailing from them. In spring 1920 the War Mothers of Houston planted 240 oak trees around the park to honor Harris County soldiers killed in World War I. Many of these trees furnish shade today.

Cross a wooden bridge that spans a portion of McGovern Lake. The 3-acre lake attracts many birds, including a variety of ducks and black cormorants. Some sections around the lake have been left unmowed to help support wildflowers and wildlife. There are benches and picnic tables here, as well as the docking area for rental paddleboats.

Go past the entrance to the Japanese garden on the left and a large graveled area on the right that has benches and lots of shade. The Mary Gibbs and Jesse H. Jones Reflecting Pool adjoins the resting area. Follow along the reflecting pool to where it ends, and turn right.

A statue of Sam Houston can be seen across Fannin Street. Continue following the trail as it curves right. The Museum of Natural Science is across the street on the left. Follow around the hill that leads to the Miller Outdoor Theatre. Continue until you reach the reflecting pool and, at its head, see the Mecom Fountain, which flows into the pool. At this point turn left and return to the parking lot.

The Hermann Park Conservancy, working in partnership with the City of Houston, has made world-class improvements to the park.

Miles and Directions

0.0 Start the wide crushed-granite trail just across the sidewalk from the parking lot at the north entrance and turn right (southwest).

0.1 Pass a sidewalk on the right that leads to Fannin Street and a Metro Train platform. Continue straight on the trail.

0.2 Reach a Y junction; take the left branch and cross over the tracks for the miniature train.

0.3 Bear left in a semicircle and pass a fenced area on the left, which is the Japanese garden.

0.5 Continue following the trail and cross a wooden bridge. Turn right (west) at the end of the bridge, and then continue straight ahead. McGovern Lake is on the right. Continue a short distance and reach another bridge. To the left is a bridge for the children's train. At the end of the bridge, bear left. The paddleboat dock area is on the right.

0.6 Follow the trail left around a small semicircle. Continue north and pass the Pioneer Memorial kiosk. Then turn right and go past the entrance to the Japanese garden.

0.7 Continue following the trail. The Mary Gibbs and Jesse H. Jones Reflecting Pool is on the right.

0.8 Reach a T intersection where the sidewalk joins the trail. Turn right (east) and follow the trail along Hermann Circle Drive. Then bear right into a semicircle and follow the trail. Cross an area of inlaid bricks with the water from the Mecom Fountain filling the reflecting pool.

0.9 The statue of Sam Houston is directly across Hermann Circle Drive and worth a short out-and-back trek to observe it. Return to the trail and head east.

1.0 Pass a sidewalk to the road on the left. The IMAX theater (part of the Houston Museum of Natural Science) and sky-scrapers can be seen on the left.

1.1 Pass numerous sidewalk paths to the street on the left and, on the right, a large grassy hill to the Miller Outdoor Theatre. Follow the trail while bearing right.

1.2 Pass a sidewalk on the right that leads to the Miller Outdoor Theatre. Continue following the trail, bearing right around the theater.

1.3 The trail surface changes to brick, with concrete sitting areas on the right and left. Continue following the trail and bearing right.

1.4 Cross a sidewalk and continue straight on the trail. The surface changes back to crushed gravel.

1.5 Reach a T intersection, with the reflecting pool and Japanese garden straight ahead. Take the right branch, heading north. The reflecting pool is adjacent to the left trail edge.

1.7 Reach a T intersection and take the left branch, heading west. Continue following the trail back toward the parking area.

1.8 Arrive back at your starting point and proceed to the parking area.

10 MacGregor Park

This tree-sheltered hike is located near the University of Houston. Particularly interesting is a group of old cedar trees, slanting at a nearly 45-degree angle. Within the park's 100 acres—donated by the MacGregor family in 1925—jumping off points are provided for several miles of hikes along Brays Bayou and lead to Memorial Park.

Distance: 1.8-mile loop
Approximate hiking time: 1 hour
Difficulty: Easy; flat paved trail
Trail surface: Asphalt, concrete
Best season: Year-round
Other trail users: Cyclists, joggers, dog walkers
Canine compatibility: Leashed dogs permitted

Fees and permits: No fees or permits required
Schedule: Dawn to dusk
Maps: USGS Park Place; park maps available at www.houston tx.gov/parks/trails.html
Trail contacts: Houston Parks & Recreation Department (HPARD); 2999 S. Wayside Dr., Houston 77023; (713) 865-4500

Finding the trailhead: From downtown Houston take I-45 to the Spur 5 exit (exit 44B) and turn right onto Spur 5. Drive 1 mile and make a slight right turn onto Wheeler Street. Turn left onto Martin Luther King Jr. Boulevard. Then turn right onto Calhoun Road and turn into the MacGregor Park parking area at 5225 Calhoun Rd. The trail is adjacent to the parking area. *DeLorme: Texas Atlas & Gazetteer:* Page134 B3. GPS: N29 42.559' / W95 20.489'

The Hike

Start the hike at the wide crushed-gravel path adjoining the south side of the parking lot, off South MacGregor Way. Turn

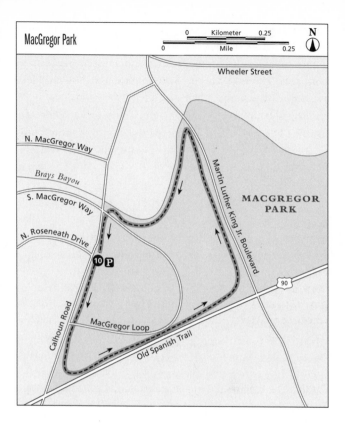

Kilometer
0   0.25
0   Mile   0.25

N

Wheeler Street

N. MacGregor Way

Brays Bayou

S. MacGregor Way

N. Roseneath Drive

MACGREGOR
PARK

Martin Luther King Jr. Boulevard

10 P

90

Calhoun Road

MacGregor Loop

Old Spanish Trail

right and come to a T. Take the left branch, passing a sign that
states OUTSIDE TRAIL—1.4 MILES / INSIDE TRAIL—1/3 MILE.

The hike is mostly through open canopy, so wear a
hat and sunscreen. The areas around the trail are grass and
mowed. Sidewalks often cross the trail, leading to the parking area, the playing fields, or the street. Benches and picnic
tables are placed conveniently near the trail.

Pass some interesting old cedar trees almost completely covered with Spanish moss that present a good photo op. There are ball fields on the left. Continue following the trail with Calhoun Road on the right, and then make a hard left, away from the road.

There are more cedar trees, but these are growing at a nearly 45-degree angle. This type of growth is more common at the Continental Divide or on windy mountaintops. It is very uncommon in the Houston area, which is barely above sea level.

Pass a series of at least ten tennis courts, for which the park is famous. Follow the trail left (north) as it parallels Martin Luther King Jr. Boulevard. Many large loblolly pines are on the left side of the trail, and several picnic shelters can be seen.

Stop at the bridge where Martin Luther King Jr. Boulevard crosses Brays Bayou. Make a hard left (west) as the trail transitions from concrete to asphalt. Walk along the bayou, which is down a slope and 45 feet away. The bayou is about 25 feet wide but subject to change depending on the amount of rainfall. It is separated from the trail by a chain-link fence. The trail generally parallels the bayou, sometimes getting closer and sometimes moving away. A stoplight at Calhoun Road and South MacGregor Way is just beyond the park entrance gate.

Turn left at this intersection and cross South MacGregor Way. *Use caution*—this street can have heavy traffic. Continue on the trail and pass a tall palm tree in front of the swimming pool building. End the hike at the entrance road to the parking area.

Miles and Directions

0.0   Start at the trailhead at the south side of the parking lot. Turn right (west) toward Calhoun Road. Almost immediately reach a T. Take the left branch, heading south.

0.1   Follow the trail as it bends slightly left with South MacGregor Way on the right, and then continue following the trail straight south.

0.3   Make a hard left bend. There is a four-lane highway (US 90) on the right. Continue following the trail east.

0.5   Pass over a sidewalk that crosses the trail from the street to the parking area.

0.7   Bear left; Martin Luther King Jr. Boulevard is straight ahead (east).

1.0   Cross South MacGregor Way as it goes to a parking area and follow the trail adjacent to Martin Luther King Jr. Boulevard.

1.2   Stop at the Martin Luther King Jr. Boulevard bridge across Brays Bayou and then make a hard left onto the asphalt trail, with the bayou on the right.

1.6   Pass the park gate and then proceed through the stoplight at Calhoun and South MacGregor. Follow the trail adjacent to Calhoun Road.

1.8   Cross the park entrance road and arrive back at the parking area.

11 Brays Bayou: Calhoun Road to Scott Street

This loop follows Brays Bayou west, on the south side of the bayou, and then returns east, on the north side of the bayou. The green space between the trail and road contains a surprising number of tree species. There are residential areas on each side of the bayou. The sides of the bayou were paved in the 1970s prior to city planners realizing natural sides do a better job.

Distance: 2.4-mile loop

Approximate hiking time: 1.2 hours

Difficulty: Easy; paved trail and level ground

Trail surface: Asphalt

Best season: September to June

Other trail users: Cyclists, joggers, dog walkers

Canine compatibility: Leashed dogs permitted

Fees and permits: No fees or permits required

Schedule: 6:00 a.m. to 11:00 p.m.

Maps: USGS Bellaire; park map available at www.co.harris.tx.us/comm_lee/

Trail contacts: Harris County Precinct One Parks Department, 7901 El Rio St., Houston 77054; (713) 440-1587

In addition: No restroom facilities or potable water available on the trail. There are facilities at MacGregor Park.

Finding the trailhead: From downtown Houston take I-45 to the Spur 5 exit (exit 44B) and turn right onto Spur 5. Drive 1 mile and make a slight right turn onto Wheeler Street. Turn left onto Martin Luther King Jr. Boulevard. Then turn right onto Calhoun Road and turn into the MacGregor Park parking area at 5225 Calhoun Rd. *DeLorme: Texas Atlas & Gazetteer:* Page 134 B3. GPS: N29 42.692' / W95 20.503'

Brays Bayou: Calhoun Road to Scott Street

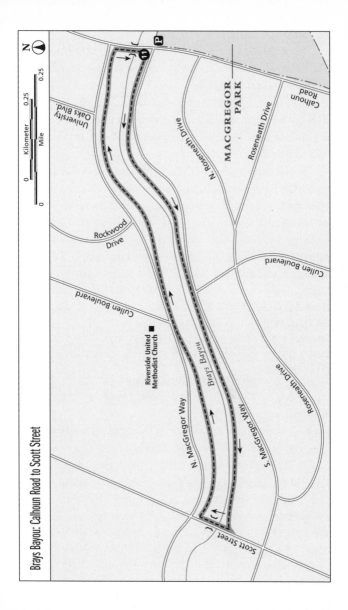

The Hike

Start the hike at the trailhead on the southwest corner of Calhoun Road and South MacGregor Way. There is no tree canopy for shade, so bring sunscreen, a hat, and water. The asphalt trail is wheelchair and stroller accessible. This is a multiuse trail, so stay to the right and be aware of cyclists and joggers.

This segment is part of the 10.2-mile Brays Bayou Hike and Bike Trail, which is part of the Harris County Precinct One park system. The bayou sides were paved during the 1970s, which eliminated most wildlife except birds. The right edge of the trail drops off steeply, going about 25 feet down to the bayou. Note the fenced and gated mini-mansions on the left (south), with their varied styles of architecture.

There are mixed hardwoods, including Shumard and live oaks, sycamore, and redbud, and scattered loblolly pines in the green space between the trail and road. Spanish moss hangs from many of the oak trees. Scan the bayou for birds. Black cormorants and white egrets enjoy the water and bayou edges. They can provide good photo ops as they look for food or just sun themselves.

Pass an area where the slope to the bayou is less steep; it goes down about 20 feet and then has a flat area before the bayou. This is an opportunity to walk down and explore the edge of the bayou, but use good sense and caution.

At the stop sign at Scott Street, turn right (north); using the pedestrian lane, cross the bridge over the bayou. Brays Bayou and the trail continue west. At the end of the bridge, turn right to complete the trail loop.

Watch for the Riverside United Methodist Church, an imposing structure, on the left. The trail is mostly straight, with a few slight bends to the right and left. The green space between the trail and road varies from 10 to 150 feet. At about 1.8 miles the trail is routed around a large live oak.

Continue following the trail east to the stop sign at Calhoun Road. University of Houston fraternity houses are across the street. Make a hard right and follow the sidewalk across the bridge to reach the trailhead.

Time and energy permitting, this hike may be combined with the adjoining MacGregor Park hike.

Miles and Directions

0.0 Start at the trailhead at the LEVI VINCENT PERRY JR. JOGGING TRAIL sign near the southwest corner of Calhoun Road and South MacGregor Way. Head west with Brays Bayou on the right and South MacGregor Way on the left.

0.2 Pass large gated and fenced mini-mansions on the left (south) side. Continue following the trail west.

0.6 Pass Cullen Boulevard on the left where it joins South MacGregor Way.

0.8 Bend slightly right and then follow the trail straight (west). You can see the Scott Street bridge over Brays Bayou.

1.2 Turn right (north) at the stop sign at Scott Street and cross the bridge over Brays Bayou. At the end of the bridge, turn right (east) back onto the trail to complete the loop. (**Option:** The Hike and Bike Trail and Brays Bayou continue west for several miles if you wish to extend the hike.)

1.5 Pass the Riverside United Methodist Church on the left (north). Continue following the trail east.

1.9 Bear slightly left and pass a solitary park bench on the left side of the trail. Continue following the trail east.

2.1 The trail jogs around a large live oak tree on the right. University Oaks Boulevard is on the left (north) where it joins North MacGregor Way.

2.3 Reach the stop sign at Calhoun Road. Make a hard right onto the sidewalk, heading south. Follow the sidewalk across the bridge and to the stop light at Calhoun Road and South MacGregor Way.

2.4 Arrive back at the trailhead.

12 John T. Mason Park

Mason Park offers hikers short, tree-filled trails on the east side of Houston. Brays Bayou flows into the park's 104 acres and then out of the park. The park's 3.5 acres of retention ponds have helped establish a wetland environment for plant and animal life. The bayou and wildlife populations add interest to the hike

Distance: 1.1-mile loop

Approximate hiking time: 45 minutes

Difficulty: Easy; paved surface and little elevation change

Trail surface: Concrete, asphalt

Best season: Year-round

Other trail users: Joggers, dog walkers

Canine compatibility: Leashed dogs permitted

Fees and permits: No fees or permits required

Schedule: Dawn to dusk

Maps: USGS Park Place; no park map available

Trail contacts: Houston Parks & Recreation Department (HPARD), 2999 S. Wayside Dr., Houston 22023; (713) 865-4500

In addition: Restroom facilities are available in the community center. Water fountains and portable toilets are located near the parking area.

Finding the trailhead: Take I-45 South toward downtown Houston. Merge onto I-10 East/US 90 East at exit 48A. Stay on I-10 to McKee Street (exit 769C) toward Hardy Street and turn right onto McKee Street. Make an easy left onto Runnels Street and then a right onto Navigation Boulevard. After 3.7 miles turn right onto South 75th Street. Turn into the John T. Mason Park, at 541 South 75th St. The trail is adjacent to the parking area. *DeLorme: Texas Atlas & Gazetteer:* Page 134 A6. GPS: N29 43.444' / W95 17.642'

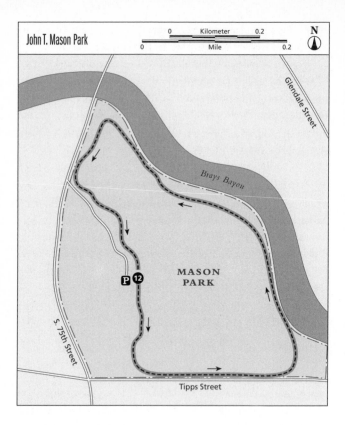

Kilometer

0   0.2

0   Mile   0.2

N

Glendale Street

Brays Bayou

MASON
PARK

P 12

S. 75th Street

Tipps Street

The Hike

There is no official trailhead for this hike. The trail is adjacent to the parking lot. Use the sidewalk from the parking
area and turn right when it T's into the wide, wheel-
chair- and stroller-accessible trail. Ball fields are on the left.
Located on Houston's east side, much of the hike is along

Brays Bayou, which enters the park at its northwest corner and then flows across the park in a southeast direction.

Brays Bayou joins Buffalo Bayou east of the park. Miles of what are called linear hike and bike trails—linear meaning they are generally out-and-back hikes—border the bayous. Many of these trails can be reached from the Mason Trail. US 90 passes the west side of the park and brings back the reality of being in the city.

The trail has a number of Y and T junctions, but all eventually lead to the section of trail along the bayou and complete the loop back to the parking area. The baseball and soccer fields are clustered near the center of the park.

In 2006 the banks of Brays Bayou were widened to reduce flooding, and 3.5 acres were developed as a series of retention ponds, creating a wetland environment. Pass the pond and bear left toward the bayou. Depending on the amount of rainfall, the pond may be empty. Loblolly pines and southern magnolia are to the left. Go down a slight slope to the bayou, where bald cypress trees have been planted near the water.

Egrets and other shorebirds can be seen in the air or near the edges of the bayou. Continue walking northwest with the bayou on the right. Watch for the place where the terrain flattens and is nearly level with the waterway. This is a great spot to do a short out-and-back trek to investigate the bayou and its rich assortment of insects and bugs. Seasonal wildflowers bloom in this area.

The bayou makes a lazy bend left and then right as it flows under the 75th Street bridge. Turn left (south) at the 75th Street bridge and continue on the sidewalk to the parking area.

In 1930 Mrs. Dora Porter Mason donated 69.88 acres

to Houston in memory of her husband. The city combined this acreage with other parcels to create 104-acre John T. Mason Park.

Miles and Directions

0.0 Start at the trailhead adjoining the parking lot and near the Spanish mission–style community center building. Turn right and follow the concrete trail north.

0.1 Reach a Y and take the right branch, heading northeast.

0.2 The asphalt trail changes to concrete just before reaching another Y. Take the right branch and follow the trail east.

0.25 Pass a retaining pond on the left and reach a Y. Take the left branch, heading north. Brays Bayou can be seen straight ahead.

0.3 Reach a T with the bayou directly ahead. Turn left and follow the trail along the bayou.

0.4 Take the right branch at a Y, following alongside the bayou. This is a good spot to go down to the edge of the bayou and then return to the trail.

0.5 Bear slightly to the left (northwest) as the bayou bends to the right and goes under the 75th Street bridge.

0.6 A narrow dirt bike path joins the trail from the left. Continue following the paved trail north.

0.7 Pass several concrete picnic tables and benches on the left.

0.8 Continue following the trail west and pass through the park entrance gate.

0.9 Turn left, heading south onto the asphalt trail next to the parking area. Continue following the trail back to the trail-head.

1.1 Arrive back at the trailhead.

13 West 11th Street Nature Trail

The West 11th Street Nature Trail is a great example of what a community nature trail should be. The trail loops through more than 1,800 trees, and more than one hundred species of birds call the park home. Only 1 block square, the park served as a community park for over fifty years before the City of Houston designated this area as a city park in 2007. This is a favorite trail for nature lovers, bird–watchers, and dog walkers.

Distance: 0.5 mile for Outer Loop Trail (1.5 miles total trails)
Approximate hiking time: 1 hour total for all trails
Difficulty: Easy; flat terrain
Trail surface: Grass, dirt
Best season: Year-round
Other trail users: Dog walkers, bird-watchers
Canine compatibility: Leashed dogs permitted
Fees and permits: No fees or permits required

Schedule: 6:00 a.m. to 11:00 p.m.
Maps: USGS Houston Heights; park maps available at www .west11thstreetpark.org/trailmap .htm
Trail contacts: Houston Parks & Recreation Department (HPARD), 2999 S. Wayside Dr., Houston 77023; (713) 865-4500; www .houstontx.gov/parks/trails.html
In addition: No toilet facilities available in the park

Finding the trailhead: From Louisiana Street, merge onto I-10 West/US 90 West. Follow I-10 for about 3 miles and take exit 765A toward T. C. Jester Boulevard. Turn right onto T. C. Jester, go about 1 mile, and turn left onto West 11th Street. The park is located at 2600 West 11th St. Park on Wister Lane, on the north side of the park, as there is no parking available within the park. There are paths

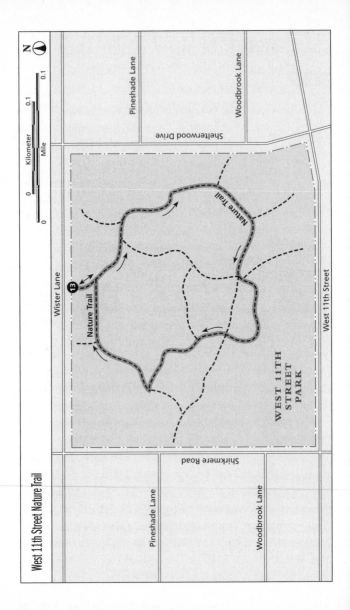

West 11th Street Nature Trail

N

Kilometer
0   0.1   0.1
0   0.1
Mile

Wister Lane

Pineshade Lane

Shelterwood Drive

Woodbrook Lane

Nature Trail

13

Nature Trail

WEST 11TH
STREET
PARK

West 11th Street

Shirkmere Road

Pineshade Lane

Woodbrook Lane

from the street to the trails. *DeLorme: Texas Atlas & Gazetteer:* Page 129 G12. GPS: N29 17.526' / W95 25.412'

The Hike

Park next to the curb on Wister Lane. There is no official trailhead, but there are seven points where you can enter the interconnecting loop trails from the four streets surrounding the park. There is no trail signage in the park.

Walk from Wister Lane to an opening in the woods and a path to the Outer Loop Trail. Almost immediately reach a T intersection. Take the left branch (east). This trail is part of the outer loop formed by the exterior edges of the four inner loops.

Look to the right (southwest) for several 60- to 70-foot-tall dead pine trunks. This area is a favorite for the red-headed woodpecker and the pileated woodpecker, which can grow larger than an American crow. Continue going straight, passing a path that joins the Outer Loop Trail from the right (southwest). This is part of the North Loop Trail. In spring, several species of colorful warblers may be seen or heard. Pass a path on the left that leads to Wister Lane. Make a hard right, heading south.

Take time to look around at the woods filled with more than 1,800 trees, including pine and many species of oak mixed with a few ash, sycamore, and elm trees. Pass a path on the left that leads to Shelterwood Drive. Bend right (southwest) at the intersection and continue a short distance, passing a path on the left leading to West 11th Street. Curve right (west) then continue straight, passing the tail of a Y crossing Outer Loop Trail. This area has tall oaks, pines, and maples that provide both shade and solitude. The maples are spectacular in fall, when their foliage turns a brilliant red.

The park is home to thirty-five species of butterflies, which may be seen at various times of the year. The black swallowtail, colored black with yellow spots, is common.

In about 200 feet a portion of the South Loop Trail crosses the Outer Loop. Make a sharp right (north), continuing to a T; take the left (west) branch. A small baseball diamond can be seen to the left. Shortly reach another T and take the right (north) branch. This is the Outer Loop Trail and returns to the starting point of the hike.

This short hike can be extended to more than 1.0 mile by taking the inner loops. The park's diversity of flora and fauna is well worth inspecting.

Miles and Directions

0.0 Start at the mowed trail off Wister Lane. Take the path into the woods and intersect the Outer Loop Trail. Turn left (east).

0.1 A path intersects from the right (south). Continue going straight (east). The path is a section of the North Loop trail. (**Option:** This intersection may be used to alter the length of the hike by taking the North Loop Trail.)

0.2 A path to Shelterwood Drive intersects the trail from the left (east). Stay on the Outer Loop Trail and bear slightly to the right (southwest).

0.25 A path to West 11th Street intersects the trail from the left (south). Bear right (west), following the Outer Loop Trail.

0.3 The tail of a Y branch intersects the trail on the left (south). The left branch of the Y is a path to West 11th Street. The right branch bears right (west) and is a short loop that reconnects with the Outer Loop Trail. The tail of the Y crosses the Outer Loop Trail and is part of the South Loop. Continue straight (west) on the Outer Loop Trail a short distance to where a section of the North Loop intersects from the left (south) and crosses the Outer Loop Trail. Make a hard right (north) onto the South Loop Trail.

0.4 Reach a T intersection. The left (southwest) branch is a portion of the Loop Trail. Take the right branch, heading northeast. This is the Outer Loop Trail and goes back to the starting point.

0.5 Arrive back at your starting point.

14 White Oak Bayou Hike and Bike Trail

This is a neighborhood hike for those who like the city environment and viewing historic Victorian architecture. This shorter section of the White Oak Hike and Bike Trail starts in Stude Park and extends from Studemont Street to Taylor Street. The trail passes ball fields, a major sculpture, and picnic areas and along White Oak Bayou. Hiking the loop presents good views of the Houston skyline and the historic Heights district.

Distance: 1.0-mile loop
Approximate hiking time: 30 minutes
Difficulty: Easy; paved trail with minor elevation changes
Trail surface: Asphalt, dirt
Best season: Year-round
Other trail users: Joggers, dog walkers
Canine compatibility: Leashed dogs permitted
Fees and permits: No fees or permits required

Schedule: 6:00 a.m. to 11:00 p.m.
Maps: USGS Houston Heights; park map available at www .houstontx.gov/parks/trails.html
Trail contacts: Houston Parks & Recreation Department (HPARD), 2999 S. Wayside Dr., Houston 77023; (713) 865-4500
In addition: There is a portable toilet on the east side of the parking area and others along the trail

Finding the trailhead: From downtown Houston take Louisiana Street to where it accesses I-10 West/US 90 West. Follow I-10 about 1.5 miles to the Taylor Street exit (exit 767B) and turn left onto Taylor Street. Follow Taylor Street to Stude Park at 2300 Taylor St. The trail adjoins the parking area. *DeLorme: Texas Atlas & Gazetteer:* Page 130 H2. GPS: N29 46.816' W95 23.029'

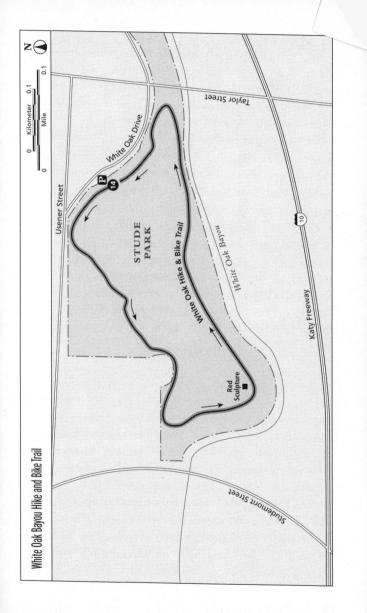

White Oak Bayou Hike and Bike Trail

The Hike

There is no marked trailhead for this hike. Start the trail as it runs parallel and adjacent to the parking area. Turn right (southeast), passing large hardwood trees including live oak and a few loblolly pines. The Houston downtown skyline can be seen across I-10. White Oak Bayou is on the south side of the park and enters the park at Studemont Street on the west and exits at Houston Avenue on the east.

This short loop furnishes good views of downtown Houston and the historic Heights district, which dates back to 1890. Oscar Martin Carter developed the neighborhood, which was 23 feet higher than downtown Houston. Carter felt the area would be a safe refuge from yellow fever and the floods that plagued the city. The Heights area still has many Victorian-style homes dating back to the turn of the twentieth century.

The trail and White Oak Bayou are bordered on the south by I-10, and this major highway with its noise and visual pollution is a vivid reminder that the hike is a "city" hike.

Hike past ball fields, park buildings, a sculpture, and picnic areas and then along the bayou. There are park benches along parts of the trail. On the first section of the hike, the bayou is to the right (south) and down a slope about 50 feet away. The sides of White Oak Bayou were hardened with concrete during the 1970s, when city planners had not yet realized the value of natural bayous.

Follow along the bayou; about halfway through the hike pass a huge red sculpture on the left. The abstract sculpture by Mac Whitney, titled *Houston,* was placed in Stude Park in 1982. The steel structure is an eye-catching 50 feet tall. Playing fields come in and out of view.

The trail gets closer to the bayou, and there is a Y junction just before Taylor Street. Take the left branch, which bears northeast and parallels White Oak Drive. There are homes and apartment complexes to the right. The hike can be extended to more than 5.0 miles along the bayou by following the right branch of the Y.

The trail makes a hard left. Look straight ahead to see a brightly painted Victorian-style home on the north side of Usener Street. This is a great photo op. Continue following the trail, with playing fields on the left and a residential community on the right. End the hike at your starting point.

Miles and Directions

0.0   Start at the trailhead at the east side of the parking area. Turn right (southwest) and pass baseball fields.

0.1   Continue straight at an inverted T intersection, then make a hard right and left.

0.2   Reach another T intersection; take the left branch, bearing south. Pass a sidewalk on the left and park buildings

0.3   Follow the trail as it makes a hard left in a semicircle. The interstate and city skyline are straight ahead. The concrete-sided bayou is down a slope about 50 feet away.

0.4   Make a hard curve left and pass a large red steel abstract sculpture. The bayou is on the right, down a slope about 40 feet. Pass the back of a park building and the swimming pool fence. The trail bears right along the bayou. Continue straight on the main trail.

0.6   Pass a playing field on the left and the bayou on the right. Go slightly down, heading east. The bayou is very close on the right. There is a playing field on the left.

0.65 Pass an apartment complex on the left.

0.75 Reach a Y just before Taylor Street. Take the left branch, heading north. (**Option:** The right branch follows along the bayou for several miles while looping back to the trailhead.)

0.8 Cross a trail; take the left side and go up a slight hill. Bear right and pass a ball field on the left. Continue straight along the chain-link fence, with a road on the right. Curve left past a brightly painted Victorian-style house straight across Usener Street.

0.9 Pass a parking area at the edge of Usener Street. Two-foot posts placed about 4 feet apart on the right separate the parking area from the trail. See city skyline to the left and behind. Pass a park bench in a shaded area on the right.

1.0 Arrive back at the trailhead.

15 Memorial Park: Purple, Yellow, Red, Blue, and Orange Loops

Combine portions of the Purple, Yellow, Red, Blue, and Orange Trails into a loop that covers the most interesting areas of the park. Memorial Park is the largest urban park in Texas, nearly double the size of New York's Central Park. Camp Logan, a World War I Army training camp, occupied this site from 1917 to 1923. The family of James Hogg (governor of Texas, 1891–95) sold 1,503 acres to the city in 1924 and later donated another 1,000 acres.

Distance: 2.4 miles of interconnecting loops

Approximate hiking time: 1.75 hours

Difficulty: Easy; forested trail with minor elevation changes

Trail surface: Crushed granite, dirt

Best season: Year-round

Other trail users: Dog walkers, mountain bikers

Canine compatibility: Leashed dogs permitted

Fees and permits: No fees or permits required

Schedule: 6:00 a.m. to 11:00 p.m.

Maps: USGS Houston Heights; park maps available at www.memorialparkconservancy.org

Trail contacts: Houston Parks & Recreation Department (HPARD), 2999 S. Wayside Dr., Houston 77023; (713) 865-4500

In addition: There is a portable toilet by the parking area and a hose for water. No potable water or restrooms are available on the trail.

Finding the trailhead: From the intersection of I-10 and I-610, take I-610 South to Memorial Drive (exit 10). Head east on Memorial Drive into the park; follow Memorial Drive to Picnic Loop and turn right. Take an immediate right into the ball field parking lot. *DeLo-*

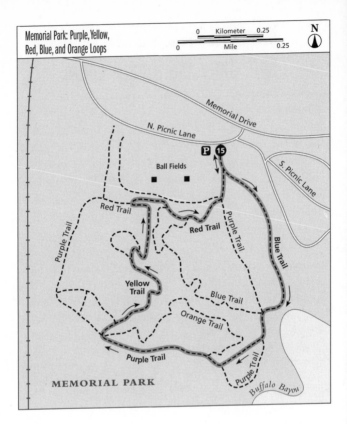

rme: Texas Atlas & Gazetteer: Page 129 I11. GPS: N29 45.883' /
W95 26.488'

The Hike

Start at the Purple Trail trailhead adjacent to the parking
area on Picnic Loop Drive. Ball fields are on the right. This
collection of trails is sometimes referred to as the Ho Chi

Minh Trail. These are among the best trails inside the I-610 loop in Houston. During spring and early fall, mosquitoes can be annoying, so be prepared.

The trail quickly veers left, away from the ball fields, and passes a path on the right, identified on a marker post as RED TRAIL. Stay on the Purple Trail, going through heavy woods that include live oak, black cherry, and loblolly pine. The path is flat, with tangled tree roots crossing it. (The Purple Trail forms a large loop back to the trailhead.)

Reach a Y junction with the Blue Trail. Follow the Blue Trail as it undulates up and down and is sometimes singletrack. There are numerous gullies, some with drop-offs of 30 feet, at the trail edge. Mountain bikers use all of these trails, so stay right and be alert. Opossums, squirrels, armadillos, raccoons, rabbits, coyotes, turtles, and snakes call this area home. Most likely only squirrels will appear, but watching for tracks can be interesting.

Stay on the Blue Trail to an intersection where a short connector dead-ends into the Purple Trail. Head south on the Purple Trail. Watch for ruby-throated hummingbirds, especially in the fall. Numerous species of birds can be seen throughout the year. In a short distance there is an intersection on the right with the Orange Trail.

Head southwest on the Orange Trail. The right edge of the trail has drop-offs into ravines; the left edge is flat. Pass some very large loblolly pines—3 feet in diameter and 80 feet tall. Reach the T where the Orange Trail dead-ends into the Purple Trail. Turn right onto the Purple Trail. Swallowtail, painted lady, and other butterflies may be seen in season.

Watch for the connector path to the Yellow Trail and follow it north. Go down a steep slope to a wooden bridge that crosses a seasonal creekbed. This section is also called the West Ridge Trail. There are some steep drop-offs going down 25 feet at the trail's edge. Some sections of the trail are singletrack. Follow a short section of the Red Trail to a T intersection where it dead-ends into the Blue Trail. Take the left branch and follow 0.2 mile to the intersection with the Purple Trail. Turn left onto the Purple Trail and back-track to the trailhead.

Miles and Directions

0.0 Start at the Purple Trail trailhead adjacent to the south end of the parking area off Picnic Loop Drive. All trails are identified with marker posts.

0.1 Pass a small path on the right (west) with a RED TRAIL marker post. Continue straight on the Purple Trail.

0.2 Reach a Y and take the left (east) branch onto the Blue Trail. The Purple Trail continues on the right branch.

0.3 Pass a BLUE TRAIL marker post on the left. Continue following the Blue Trail in a generally southern direction.

0.4 The trail zigzags through the woods, sometimes bending hard left and then hard right.

0.5 Reach a T and take the left branch onto the Purple Trail, heading southeast.

0.6 Reach a chain-link fence blocking mountain bikers. Bear slightly left at the T to get around the fence and then continue straight on the Purple Trail.

0.7 Make a hard left, travel down a slope, and then pass over a culvert. Reach a Y and take the right branch onto the Orange Trail, heading southwest. Continue following the Orange Trail.

0.9 Reach a T where the Orange Trail dead-ends into the Purple Trail. Turn right, following the right branch west. Continue following the Purple Trail.

1.1 Reach a junction with the Purple Trail continuing straight (west by northwest), a connector path to the Yellow Trail on the right, and the Orange Trail on the right. Take the connector path, heading north to the Yellow Trail.

1.2 Follow the connector path to where it T's with the Yellow Trail. Take the right branch, heading northeast. (FYI: This is also called the West Ridge Trail.)

1.4 Pass a YELLOW TRAIL marker post on the left. Continue following the Yellow Trail in a generally north direction.

1.7 Pass a YELLOW TRAIL marker post on the right. Continue following the Yellow Trail north.

1.9 Reach a junction where the Yellow Trail dead-ends at the Purple Trail, with the Red Trail on the right. Turn hard right onto the Red Trail and immediately reach a Y junction. Take the right branch, heading east. (FYI: The left branch is also the Red Trail.)

2.0 Continue straight (east), following the Red Trail. Pass an intersection on the left that is also a section of the Red Trail.

2.1 Reach a T intersection where the Red Trail dead-ends into the Blue Trail. Take the left branch, heading east on the Blue Trail.

2.3 Reach a junction where the Blue Trail crosses the Purple Trail. Turn left (north) onto the Purple Trail and backtrack the short distance to the trailhead.

2.4 Arrive back at the Purple Trail trailhead and return to the parking lot.

16 Houston Arboretum: Outer Loop

This well-marked loop trail skirts the perimeter of the park and gives a taste of the variety of the arboretum's flora and fauna. A short out-and-back path leads to Buffalo Bayou and a bird-watching platform. Depending on the season, you might see an alligator near the bayou. This area has perfect habitat for birds, mammals, and snakes. The nature center at the trailhead is well worth visiting for its displays and hands-on exhibits.

Distance: 2.5-mile loop
Approximate hiking time: 1.5 hours
Difficulty: Easy; flat terrain
Trail surface: Packed crushed gravel, boardwalks, dirt
Best season: Year-round
Other trail users: Dog walkers, bird-watchers
Canine compatibility: Leashed dogs permitted
Fees and permits: No fees or permits required; donations accepted to cover operating costs
Schedule: 8:30 a.m. to 6:00 p.m.

Maps: USGS Houston Heights; maps available in the park and at www.houstonarboretum.org
Trail contacts: Houston Arboretum and Nature Center, 4501 Woodway Dr., Houston 77024-7708; (713) 681-8433
In addition: Restrooms and water are available at the visitor center. Joggers and cyclists are not allowed on arboretum trails. To protect wildlife, no picnicking or eating is allowed in the park. Houston Arboretum and Nature Center is a nonprofit organization that uses contributions to help meet operating expenses.

Finding the trailhead: From the intersection of I-10 and I-610 South, take the I-610 loop South to Memorial Drive/Woodway Drive (exit 10). Turn left at Woodway Drive and into the arboretum parking area at 4501 Woodway Dr. Parking is at the visitor center, along

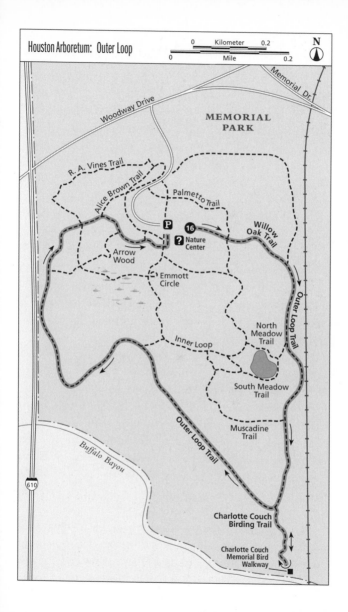

Houston Arboretum: Outer Loop

MEMORIAL PARK

Woodway Drive

Memorial Dr.

R. A. Vines Trail

Alice Brown Trail

Palmetto Trail

Willow Oak Trail

P

16

? Nature Center

Arrow Wood

Emmott Circle

Outer Loop Trail

North Meadow Trail

Inner Loop

South Meadow Trail

Muscadine Trail

Buffalo Bayou

610

Outer Loop Trail

Charlotte Couch Birding Trail

Charlotte Couch Memorial Bird Walkway

N

Kilometer
0   0.2

Mile
0   0.2

the central driveway as you enter the park. The trailhead adjoins the parking area. *DeLorme: Texas Atlas & Gazetteer:* Page 129 J10. GPS: N29 45.928' / W95 27.096'

The Hike

Start the hike at the Willow Oak trailhead, located adjacent to the east end of the parking area. Head east toward the Outer Loop Trail. This hike combines sections of the Willow Oak, Outer Loop, and Alice Brown Trails and the out-and-back Charlotte Couch Birding Trail.

All the trails are well marked, so it is easy to alter any hike as you go. Another advantage is that most of the trails are short, ranging in length from 0.08 mile to 0.5 mile. Many boardwalks, mulch, and leaf-covered dirt make up the trails' surface. Benches are placed strategically along the trails and are generally in the shade. Much of the hike is in the woods and well shaded, passing through forest, pond, and meadow habitats.

On the east side of the park, the Outer Loop Trail skirts the edge of a demonstration meadow. It consists of mostly grasses, sedges (rushlike plants), and wildflowers. Watch for sunflowers, asters, coreopsis, and the Texas paintbrush, looking like a ragged brush dipped in bright paint.

This is a great place to watch for some of the 167 species of birds found in the park, including killdeers, swallows, Carolina wrens, and the colorful eastern bluebirds. Red-tailed hawks may be observed perched in a tree watching for a meal.

Nonvenomous water snakes reside near the pond, including the black-banded water snake, which is often mistaken for a water moccasin. Venomous water moccasins do live in the park, but when found they are moved to the bayou area. In spring listen for the sounds of green tree frogs as groups of them form a noisy chorus.

Coyotes have moved into the park and are breeding here. It is unusual to see one, but watching for their tracks adds interest to the hike. They are similar to a dog's print, except the coyote's front paw print is slightly larger than its back and shows four toes, while the back print is shaped like a pair of lips.

At the Charlotte Couch Bird Walkway overlooking Buffalo Bayou—at the end of the out-and-back leg of the hike—you might spot herons, egrets, and numerous song-birds. River birch, dogwoods, and a variety of other tree species can be seen.

Return to the Outer Loop and watch for southern red oaks, post oaks, large loblolly pines, and southern magnolias and numerous songbirds flitting in and out of the woods. Add another dimension to this hike by taking along binoculars or a field guide of your choice.

Miles and Directions

NOTE: All arboretum trails are clearly identified with marker posts.

0.0 Start at the Willow Oak trailhead at the east side of the parking area. Head due east on the trail.

0.1 In less than 0.1 mile reach the junction with the Palmetto Trail, which crosses Willow Oak from north to south. Continue east on Willow Oak.

0.2 In less than 0.2 mile reach the T where Willow Oak Trail ends at the Outer Loop Trail. Turn right onto the Outer Loop Trail and follow it south.

0.4 Bear left (east) and pass the North Meadow Trail on the right. Continue following the Outer Loop Trail around the meadow on the right, heading southeast and then bearing south.

0.5 Continue on the Outer Loop Trail as it passes the South Meadow Trail to the right (west). A sign states TO POND.

0.6 Continue following the Outer Loop Trail south and pass the Muscadine Trail on the right (west). Bear slightly left (east) while following the Outer Loop.

0.8 Reach a wooden bench and sign on the left for the Charlotte Couch Birding Trail. Turn left onto the narrow out-and-back path, heading southeast.

1.0 Reach a boardwalk that leads up to the Charlotte Couch Memorial Bird Walkway. The wooden platform overlooks Buffalo Bayou. A sign warns of the presence of alligators. Backtrack to where you left the Outer Loop.

1.2 Reach the T with the Outer Loop Trail and turn left, heading west. Follow the trail as it bends left (northwest).

1.4 Pass a semicircular clearing on the right that is about 60 feet across and 30 feet deep.

1.7 Reach a junction on the right where a short connector trail leads east to the Inner Loop Trail. Continue on the Outer Loop Trail, making a sweeping semicircle to the left, heading southwest, and then bend right heading north.

2.1 Reach a junction on the right (east) where Arrow Wood Trail T's into the Outer Loop. Continue following the Outer Loop Trail as it heads north and then bends hard right, heading east.

2.3 Reach the junction where the R. A. Vines Trail crosses the Outer Loop from north to south. Continue following the Outer Loop as it bears east.

2.4 Reach the junction where the Alice Brown Trail crosses the Outer Loop. Turn right onto the Alice Brown Trail, heading southeast. Cross the Arrow Wood Trail and continue following the Alice Brown Trail.

2.5 End the hike at the back of the visitor center and arrive back at the parking area.

17 Houston Arboretum: Inner Loops

This hike is great for nature lovers and families. Several well-marked interconnecting loops pass by a small pond full of life, over boardwalks, and through a swamp, heavy woods, and a meadow area. This is the perfect habitat for birds, mammals, and snakes. The park is on the site of Camp Logan, which was active in 1917 during World War I. Armadillos occasionally dig up Camp Logan artifacts while searching for food.

Distance: 1.4 miles of interconnecting loops

Approximate hiking time: 1 hour

Difficulty: Easy; level terrain

Trail surface: Boardwalks, packed gravel, mulch, dirt

Best season: Year-round

Other trail users: Bird-watchers, dog walkers

Canine compatibility: Leashed dogs permitted

Fees and permits: No fees or permits required; donations accepted to cover operating costs

Schedule: 8:30 a.m. to 6:00 p.m. in winter; 8:30 a.m. to 8:00 p.m. in summer

Maps: USGS Houston Heights; excellent trail maps available at the visitor center for a minimal contribution; maps also available at www.houstonarboretum.org/hours.asp and www.houston arboretum.org/propertymap.asp

Trail contacts: Houston Arboretum and Nature Center, 4501 Woodway Dr., Houston 77024-7708; (713) 681-8433

In addition: Restrooms and water are available at the visitor center. Joggers and cyclists are not allowed on arboretum trails. To protect wildlife, no picnicking or eating is allowed in the park. Houston Arboretum and Nature Center is a nonprofit organization that uses contributions to meet operating expenses.

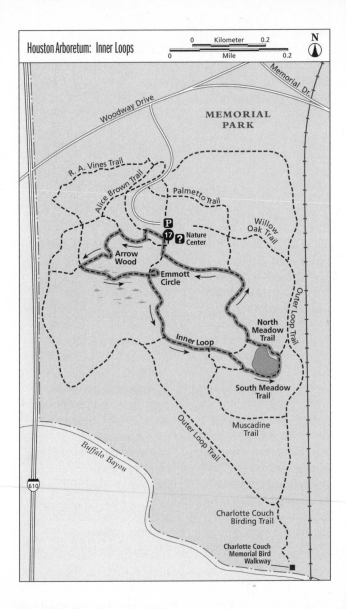

Houston Arboretum: Inner Loops

N

0   Kilometer   0.2
0   Mile   0.2

Woodway Drive

Memorial Dr.

MEMORIAL PARK

R. A. Vines Trail

Alice Brown Trail

Palmetto Trail

Willow Oak Trail

P
17
Nature Center
?

Arrow Wood

Emmott Circle

North Meadow Trail

Inner Loop

South Meadow Trail

Outer Loop Trail

Muscadine Trail

Buffalo Bayou

610

Outer Loop Trail

Charlotte Couch Birding Trail

Charlotte Couch Memorial Bird Walkway

Finding the trailhead: From the intersection of I-10 and I-610 South, take I-610 South to Memorial Drive/Woodway Drive (exit 10). Turn left at Woodway Drive and into the parking area at 4501 Woodway Dr. Parking is along the central driveway at the visitor center. The trailhead is at the rear of the nature center. *DeLorme: Texas Atlas & Gazetteer:* Page 129 K11. GPS: N29 45.904' / W95 22.127'

The Hike

After picking up a trail map, start this hike behind the nature center at the Alice Brown trailhead. This portion of the hike is wheelchair and stroller accessible. Benches are placed strategically and are generally in the shade. Much of the hike is in the woods and well shaded. In spring and early fall, mosquitoes can be pesky, so be prepared.

Portions of the Alice Brown, Arrow Wood, R. A. Vines, and Inner Loop Trails will be explored. All the trails are well marked, so it is easy to alter the hike as you go. The swamp area, reached on the R. A. Vines Trail, teems with wildlife. The trail is named in honor of Robert A. Vines, a local ecologist who during the 1950s advocated using a section of a Memorial Park as a nature sanctuary.

Enjoy the sounds of the swamp, including the deep "jug-o-rum" of the bullfrog, the largest frog in North America. Red-eared slider turtles may be basking on logs and will quickly slide into the water when they sense vibrations from walkers.

Watch for dragonflies as they hover in one spot while hunting for mosquitoes. Ribbon snakes, which may reach 2 feet in length, like to be near the water's edge. These non-venomous, fast-moving snakes feast on salamanders, frogs, and insects. Nonvenomous broad-banded water snakes, often mistaken for venomous water moccasins, swim in the water. The park staff removes any water moccasins they find from the trails to the area around the bayou. The swamp cyrilla thrives in the wet conditions. The shrub stays green most of the year and produces little white flowers that have a lot of nectar to attract bees.

On the Inner Loop Trail listen for the drumming of woodpeckers. Watch for the six species of these colorful birds found in the park, ranging from the size of a small fist to the size of a crow. There are 167 species of birds in the park.

This trail presents a good sampling of the more than one hundred species of trees and shrubs growing in the park. Oaks are common. Twelve species are represented, including evergreen, live, southern red, and post oaks. Make a game out of trying to identify the acorns. Pass loblolly pines, dogwoods, ashes, magnolias, and sycamores. Add another dimension to the hike by taking along your favorite field guide.

Miles and Directions

0.0   Start at the sidewalk in the rear of the nature center. Then follow the boardwalk through several displays.

0.1   Reach a Y at the Alice Brown trailhead; take the left branch, heading south, and then bear right (west).

0.2   Reach a junction where Arrow Wood Trail crosses the Alice Brown Trail. Turn left, going south on the Arrow Wood Trail.

0.25 Pass a small pond on the left surrounded by a boardwalk. Continue south on the Arrow Wood Trail.

0.3   Reach a junction with the R. A. Vines Trail. Turn left (east) onto the R. A. Vines and follow the trail and boardwalks through the swamp area.

0.5   Reach a junction with the Inner Loop Trail. Continue following the R. A. Vines Trail across the Inner Loop Trail and follow left around Emmott Circle back to the junction. Go left onto the Inner Loop Trail, heading south.

0.6   Pass a connector path on the right to the Outer Loop Trail. Bear left, following the Inner Loop east.

0.7   Pass a connector path on the right to the Muscadine Trail. Continue following the Inner Loop east.

0.8   Reach a Y and take the right branch onto the South Meadow Trail, heading southeast.

0.9   Bear left on the trail and pass a pond with a boardwalk. Follow as the trail turns and heads north to a T. South Meadow Trail ends at the T. Take the left branch west onto North Meadow Trail.

1.0   Reach a T where North Meadow ends. Take the right branch, heading north onto the Inner Loop Trail.

1.2   Bear left (west) before reaching a junction on the right where Palmetto Trail dead-ends into the Inner Loop Trail. Continue heading west on the Inner Loop.

1.3   Turn right onto a connector path that leads north, back to the nature center.

1.4   Arrive back at the rear of the nature center.

18 Buffalo Bayou: Tinsley Trail

This hike has a split personality. The Houston skyline is to the north. Allen Parkway and Memorial Drive serve as north and south borders, and in between is the park with a large greenbelt area and Buffalo Bayou meandering through it. Sections of the hike offer a retreat from the hustle and bustle of the city while still within it.

Distance: 2.4 miles out and back
Approximate hiking time: 1.5 hours
Difficulty: Easy; paved trail with minor elevation changes
Trail surface: Concrete, asphalt
Best season: Year-round
Other trail users: Dog walkers, joggers, cyclists
Canine compatibility: Leashed dogs permitted
Fees and permits: No fees or permits required
Schedule: 6:00 a.m. to 11:00 p.m.

Maps: USGS Houston Heights; no maps available in the park
Trail contacts: Houston Parks & Recreation Department (HPARD), 2999 S. Wayside Dr., Houston 77023; (713) 865-4500; www .houstontx.gov/parks/trails.html
In addition: Many high-attendance events are held in the park. Call in advance for a schedule—the park will be crowded and parking difficult. There are no restrooms along the trail.

Finding the trailhead: Traveling south on I-45 toward downtown Houston, take the Allen Parkway exit (47A) on the left. Pass Sabine Street; the park entrance is immediately on the right. Turn right into the parking lot at 500 Allen Parkway. *DeLorme: Texas Atlas & Gazetteer:* Page 130 J2. GPS: N29 45.702' / W95 22.758'

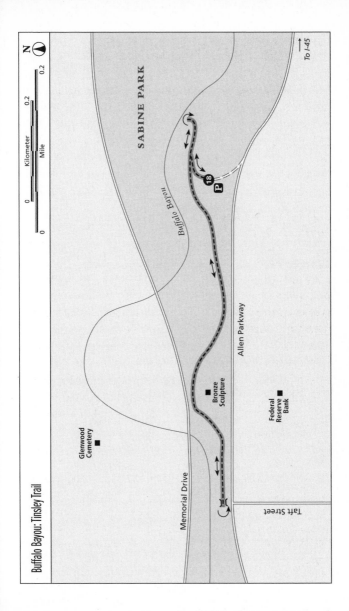

Buffalo Bayou: Tinsley Trail

SABINE PARK

Buffalo Bayou

Glenwood
Cemetery

Bronze
Sculpture

Federal
Reserve
Bank

Memorial Drive

Allen Parkway

Taft Street

18
P

To I-45

N

Kilometer
0   0.2

Mile
0   0.2

The Hike

Eleanor Tinsley Park is located southwest of downtown Houston, within the Sabine-to-Taft Greenway. The trailhead is located off the northeast corner of the parking lot. The park is the site of major festivals and events, including the city's Fourth of July fireworks extravaganza.

Start at the sidewalk with a short out-and-back down to the bayou. Follow the trail as it slopes down and doubles back on itself, then straightens out and leads to the edge of the water. There is a landing from which canoes may be launched. Interesting retaining walls, made from stone, follow the slope. There is a children's playground in the green space.

Backtrack and follow the sidewalk west, to the sign at the trailhead marked BIKE ROUTE. This is a multiuse trail, so stay to the right and be alert to cyclists. Buffalo Bayou is down a slope to the right; Allen Parkway is on the left. Trees line Allen Parkway, including some large live oaks, but the traffic noise can be distracting.

The interior of the park consists of green space, mostly mowed grass, and many trees, including oak, sycamore, and magnolia. The bayou meanders through the center. Benches are placed along the trail. This is one of a few hikes with fire hydrants along the trail. Now that's different!

The trail passes through open and shaded tree canopy. The bayou is to the right and generally about 40 feet away, down a slope. In some sections it's possible to get to the edge of the bayou. When backtracking, great views of downtown Houston are available.

Pass a large sculpture on the left, *Large Spindle Piece,* a 12-foot-tall abstract bronze by Henry Moore (1898–1986).

Originally located in London's Hyde Park, the sculpture was purchased by the Knox Foundation and given to the city in 1979.

Pass an imposing brown structure on the left, across Allen Parkway. This is the Houston branch of the Federal Reserve Bank. The 9-acre complex consists of seven buildings.

The Police Officers Memorial can be seen to the right, across Memorial Drive. The pyramid-shaped concrete monument is Mayan inspired, and a pool of bubbling water flows down from the top.

The park is named in honor of city councilwoman Eleanor Tinsley, who served from 1980 to 1990.

Miles and Directions

0.0 Start at the trailhead adjacent to the northeast side of the Tinsley Park parking area.

0.1 Continue following the trail (sidewalk) as it bends back on itself and slopes down toward the bayou.

0.2 Reach the bank of Buffalo Bayou. (FYI: Canoes may be launched from this point.) Backtrack to the trailhead and parking area to continue the hike.

0.3 Reach trailhead and follow trail right to the BIKE ROUTE sign. Allen Parkway is on the left, about 60 feet away.

0.5 Continue following the concrete trail west. Allen Parkway is on the left, with green space and the bayou visible on the right.

0.6 Continue following the trail as it bends right, away from Allen Parkway.

0.7 The trail changes from concrete sidewalk to asphalt. The trail bears toward the bayou on the right. The *Large Spindle Piece* sculpture is on the left.

0.9 The imposing Federal Reserve Bank building is directly across Allen Parkway.

1.0 The trail passes the television Channel 11 (KHOU) building on the left (south), with a helicopter landing pad on its roof.

1.2 Cross the Taft Tributary, which flows into Buffalo Bayou, on a short footbridge. Bear right, heading north for a short way.

1.4 Heading west on the trail, pass under a concrete bridge at Taft Avenue. The trail continues west, but instead backtrack for 0.3 mile.

1.7 Stop backtracking and bear left (northeast) of the concrete trail onto a narrow dirt trail created by cyclists. This path follows the south edge of the bayou.

1.8 Follow the bike path along the bayou and up a slope to rejoin the concrete trail. Backtrack to the trailhead.

2.4 Arrive back at the trailhead and parking area.

19 Buffalo Bayou: Blue Lagoon Trail

This downtown trail is located in the 23-acre Sabine-to-Bagby Waterfront Park. Due to its signature lighting system, this is a trail that is best to hike at night. The lights change colors from white to blue based on the phases of the moon. Much of the hike is below street level and passes the Theater District as it explores both sides of Buffalo Bayou.

Distance: 2.4 mile out and back with a small loop
Approximate hiking time: 1.5 hours
Difficulty: Easy; paved surface and some stairs
Trail surface: Concrete
Best season: Year-round
Other trail users: Dog walkers, cyclists, tourists
Canine compatibility: Leashed dogs permitted
Fees and permits: No fees or permits required

Schedule: 6:00 a.m. to 11:00 p.m.
Maps: USGS Settegast; park map available at www.buffalo bayou.org/sabinebagby.html
Trail contacts: Houston Parks & Recreation Department (HPARD), 2999 S. Wayside Dr., Houston 77023; (713) 865-4500; www .houstontx.gov/parks/trails.html
In addition: There are no restroom facilities on the hike, but the aquarium complex allows hikers to use their restrooms.

Finding the trailhead: Traveling south on I-45 toward downtown Houston, take the Allen Parkway exit (47A) on the left. Turn right onto Sabine Street; go 1 block and then turn right onto Memorial Drive. Continue half a block to city parking lot H. *DeLorme: Texas Atlas & Gazetteer:* Page 130 J2. GPS: N29 45.754' / W95 22.441'

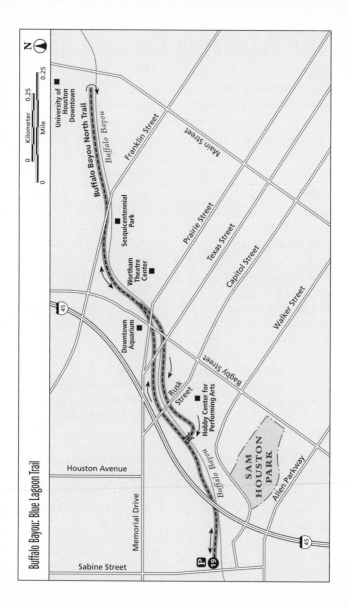

Buffalo Bayou: Blue Lagoon Trail

N

0 Kilometer 0.25

0 Mile 0.25

■ University of Houston Downtown

Buffalo Bayou North Trail

Buffalo Bayou

Franklin Street

Main Street

Prairie Street

Texas Street

Capitol Street

Walker Street

■ Sesquicentennial Park

■ Wortham Theatre Center

■ Downtown Aquarium

45

Bagby Street

Rusk Street

■ Hobby Center for Performing Arts

Buffalo Bayou

SAM HOUSTON PARK

Allen Parkway

Houston Avenue

Memorial Drive

Sabine Street

45

P
19

The Hike

Start the hike from city parking lot H. The Blue Bayou Trail, aka the Sabine-to-Bagby Promenade, was opened in June 2006. Much of the trail is wheelchair and stroller accessible. This is a multiuse trail, so stay to the right and watch for cyclists and joggers. There are benches along the trail.

The trail's signature element is the cobalt blue and white lights that line its entire length and at night illuminate the bayou. The lights shift with the phases of the moon. On each full moon all lights are white. Then, traveling from east to west, the lights change to blue until they are all blue for the new moon. There's also blue and white lighting of the trees, which makes for a spectacular visual. This lighting created a new opportunity for hiking at night.

Daytime hiking is also visually pleasant due to 300,000 plants and 600 native trees that line the banks of the bayou. The trail weaves through willows, oaks, river birch, sycamore, magnolia, dogwood, and many other tree species. Attention-getting shrubs and groundcover reach down to the edge of the water. Birds, including songbirds and white egrets, enjoy the water. Sections of the trail are below I-45, which furnishes additional shade—and noise.

The trail has five entries, called portals, which invite hikers into the park. Each portal has a raised 20-foot stainless-steel, upside-down canoe sculpture that serves as a bayou landmark. Folks can walk under it as they enter the park. Now that's something different!

The Downtown Aquarium, located just before the Bagby Street bridge, features a 500,000-gallon aquarium, dining venues, and an amusement park. The aquarium is located on the north side of the bayou and can be reached from the trail. The Entertainment District is on the south side of the bayou and includes the Wortham Center, where the Houston Ballet and Grand Opera perform. The Hobby Center for the Performing Arts is also on the south side.

The pedestrian bridge, 189 feet long and 10 feet wide, has plenty of space for hikers, joggers, cyclists, and tourists. It provides access to both banks of the bayou without having to cross any streets. The view from the center of the bridge provides a good photo op.

After reaching the University of Houston, enjoy a great view of downtown. Then backtrack to the trailhead, possibly stopping to enjoy a meal along the way.

Miles and Directions

0.0 Start at the Buffalo Bayou North Trail connector path at the sign at the southeast corner of city parking lot H. Turn left (east) at the T intersection.

0.1 Pass a brick path on the right that leads to the edge of the bayou. I-45 is directly overhead.

0.2 Reach a Y junction and take the right branch, labeled LOWER TRAIL. This is closer to the bayou and will reconnect with the left branch. It also passes under the 189-foot-long wooden pedestrian bridge that connects both sides of the bayou.

0.3 Pass a portal (entrance) with stairs leading to Memorial Drive. The "upside-down canoe" is visible.

0.4 Pass a stairway on the right leading down to the bayou.

0.5 Pass a stairway on the left leading up to the Downtown Aquarium entertainment complex. Restrooms and water are available at the complex.

0.6 Reach a Y. Take the right branch, which leads under the Bagby Street bridge. This is the end of the Blue Bayou Trail and its lights. Sesquicentennial Park begins at this point.

0.7 Cross a short wooden bridge over a drainage channel that leads to the bayou. Continue following the trail.

0.8 Go under a bridge and bear left, following the trail.

0.9 I-45 is above the trail, and there are many concrete support pilings around the trail.

1.0 You can see the University of Houston–Downtown immediately ahead. The Spaghetti Warehouse is to the right and ahead.

1.2 The trail ends at the University of Houston, which is on the left. Go up seven flights of stairs to the street-level University Plaza. The view of downtown Houston is great. Backtrack to the Bagby Street bridge and the portal to the street.

1.8 Cross the bridge to the south side of Buffalo Bayou. Turn right and follow the Blue Bayou Trail. The bayou is on the right, and the Downtown Aquarium is across the bayou.

2.0 Pass under the Capitol Street bridge and stairs on the left leading up to Capitol Street.

2.1 The Hobby Center parking building is on the left.

2.2 Reach the wooden pedestrian bridge. Turn right onto the bridge and cross over the bayou to the Upper Trail. Turn left onto the Upper Trail and backtrack to the trailhead.

2.4 Arrive back at the trailhead and return to city parking lot H.

20 Buffalo Bayou: Sabine Street to Waugh Street

Explore 2 miles on the north side of Buffalo Bayou, just west of downtown Houston. Good views of the downtown skyline are available. There is much green space, and the bayou's edges support a wide variety of tree species. Along the way you'll reach the Waugh Street bridge, home to 250,000 Mexican free-tailed bats. Year-round residents, the bats can be observed leaving their roost around dusk.

Distance: 4.4 miles out and back

Approximate hiking time: 2.75 hours

Difficulty: Easy due to paved trail; little elevation change

Trail surface: Asphalt, concrete

Best season: Year-round

Other trail users: Cyclists, joggers, dog walkers

Canine compatibility: Leashed dogs permitted

Fees and permits: No fees or permits required

Schedule: 6:00 a.m. to 11:00 p.m.

Maps: USGS Settegast; no maps available in the park

Trail contacts: Houston Parks & Recreation Department (HPARD), 2999 S. Wayside Dr., Houston 77023; (713) 865-4500; www.houstontx.gov/parks/trails.html

In addition: There are no restroom facilities on the trail.

Finding the trailhead: Traveling north on I-45 toward downtown Houston, take the Allen Parkway exit (47A) on the left. Turn right onto Sabine Street and then right onto Memorial Drive and continue to city parking lot H. *DeLorme: Texas Atlas & Gazetteer:* Page 130 J2. GPS: N29 45.754' / W95 22.441'

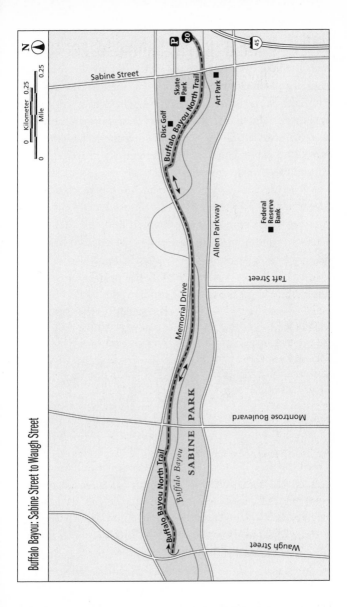

Buffalo Bayou: Sabine Street to Waugh Street

The Hike

Start the hike from city parking lot H. Follow the connector path at the southeast corner to the T intersection and take the right (west) branch. The trail is wheelchair and stroller accessible. This is a multiuse trail, so stay to the right and watch for cyclists and joggers. There are benches along the trail. The tree canopy is intermittent but furnishes some shade. Take a hat, sunscreen, and water.

This very short part of the trail, until it reaches Sabine Street, is technically part of the Blue Bayou Trail. Enter the Art Park, a small grassy area around the trail where sculptures and other artwork from local artists are displayed. The sidewalk sections are painted alternately blue and white, displaying a poem. Reach the portal (entrance) to Sabine Street. At the entrance on the right, a raised 20-foot stainless-steel, upside-down canoe sculpture that serves as a bayou landmark can be seen. Continue west, going under the Sabine Street bridge.

The left edge of the trail slopes down about 25 feet to the bayou. To the right and left of the trail, the green space is mostly mowed grass, with bushes and trees at the water's edge. Eleanor Tinsley Park can be seen to the left, across the bayou. Up a slope and on the right side is the Lee and Joe Jamail Skate Park; adjoining it is the Jim Mozola Memorial Disc Golf area. The trail follows the bayou as it makes a lazy bend to the right. Willows, live oaks, sycamores, and other trees line the water's edge.

Reach a sidewalk on the right and follow it, making a short out-and-back walk into a small section of woods. There is a drainage channel lined with rocks and concrete leading to the bayou. Maidenhair ferns and wildflowers create a pleasant palette. Benches and large rocks are available to sit on. This peaceful, shaded area is a great spot for a snack. Backtrack to the main trail and turn right.

Continue following the curves and bends as the trail heads west. On the right is a large group of live oak trees with their branches touching the ground. Inhale—but not too deeply. The slightly unpleasant aroma is from the guano (droppings) of the 250,000 Mexican free-tailed bats that roost under the Waugh Street bridge. This is a good spot to stop and backtrack to the trailhead.

Miles and Directions

0.0 Start at the Buffalo Bayou North Trail connector path at the sign at the southeast corner of city parking lot H. Turn right (west) onto the trail at the T intersection.

0.1 Go through the Art Park with a few scattered exhibits. Pass the portal (entrance) on the right with stairs to Sabine Street. Continue following the trail and pass under the Sabine Street bridge.

0.2 Pass the Lee and Joe Jamail Skate Park and the Jim Mozola Memorial Disc Golf area, both on the right.

0.4 Turn right where a sidewalk joins the trail for a short out-and-back walk in the woods. Stop before reaching the buildings and backtrack.

0.5 Reach the T intersection at the main trail; turn right (west) and follow the trail.

0.6 Reach and cross a short wooden footbridge over the Tapley Tributary, which flows to the bayou.

0.9 Bend left in a semicircle and follow along the bayou. The imposing three-story brown Federal Reserve Bank building can be seen directly to the left, across the bayou and Allen Parkway.

1.0 Continue west on the trail, and on the left side pass the back of the Police Memorial.

1.1 Bend to the right, away from the bayou, and go under the Memorial Drive bridge.

1.2 Reach a bike path joining the trail on the left. The bridge is still above. Turn left (south) onto the bike path as it leads away from bridge to the bayou; then bear right (west) and follow the path until it joins the main trail.

1.3 Reach the main trail coming from the right and continue west.

1.7 Continue following the trail west. Pass under a bridge crossing the bayou, joining Allen Parkway and Memorial Drive.

1.9 Continue following the trail west. Pass a bench and exercise station with a chinning bar. Then cross a wooden platform bridge over a tributary to Buffalo Bayou.

2.1 Bear left (south), then straight ahead, and then right (west). The Waugh Street bridge is in view. There is a water fountain to the right of the trail.

2.2 Pass a group of very large live oaks on the left. Reach the Waugh Street bridge, home to 250,000 bats! Stop at this point and backtrack to the trailhead.

4.4 Arrive back at the trailhead and return to city parking lot H.

Houston Area Hiking Clubs

Sierra Club Houston Group
P.O. Box 3021
Houston 77253-3021
(713) 895-9309
www.houston.sierraclub.org

Houston Happy Hikers
(979) 478-6203
www.houstonhappyhikers.org

Lone Star Hiking Trail Club
113 Ben Drive
Houston 77022
www.lshtclub.com

The Woodlands Hiking Club
www.woodlandshikingclub.com

The Art of Hiking

When standing nose to nose with a mountain lion, you're probably not too concerned with the issue of ethical behavior in the wild. No doubt you're just terrified. But let's be honest. How often are you nose to nose with a mountain lion? For most of us, a hike into the "wild" means loading up the SUV with expensive gear and driving to a toileted trailhead. Sure, you can mourn how civilized we've become—how GPS units have replaced natural instinct and Gore-Tex, true-grit—but the silly gadgets of civilization aside, we have plenty of reason to take pride in how we've matured. With survival now on the back burner, we've begun to reason—and it's about time—that we have a responsibility to protect, no longer just conquer, our wild places: that they, not we, are at risk. So please, do what you can. The following section will help you understand better what it means to "do what you can" while still making the most of your hiking experience. Anyone can take a hike, but hiking safely and well is an art requiring preparation and proper equipment.

Preparedness

It's been said that failing to plan means planning to fail. So do take the necessary time to plan your trip. Whether going on a short day hike or an extended backpack trip, always prepare for the worst. Simply remembering to pack a copy of the U.S. Army Survival Manual is not preparedness. Although it's not a bad idea if you plan on entering truly wild places, it's merely the tourniquet answer to a problem. You need to do your best to prevent the problem from arising in the first place. In order to survive—and to stay reasonably comfortable—you need to concern yourself with the basics: water, food, and shelter. Don't go on a hike without having these bases covered. And don't go on a hike expecting to find these items in the woods.

Water. Even in frigid conditions, you need at least two quarts of water a day to function efficiently. Add heat and taxing terrain and you can bump that figure up to one gallon. That's simply a base to work from—your metabolism and your level of conditioning can raise or lower that amount. Unless you know your level, assume that you need one gallon of water a day. Now, where do you plan on getting the water?

Preferably not from natural water sources. These sources can be loaded with intestinal disturbers, such as bacteria, viruses, and fertilizers. *Giardia lamblia,* the most common of these disturbers, is a protozoan parasite that lives part of its life cycle as a cyst in water sources. The parasite spreads when mammals defecate in water sources. Once ingested, Giardia can induce cramping, diarrhea, vomiting, and fatigue within two days to two weeks after ingestion. Giardiasis is treatable with prescription drugs. If you believe you've contracted giardiasis, see a doctor immediately.

Dehydration. Have you ever hiked in hot weather and had a roaring headache and felt fatigued after only a few miles? More than likely you were dehydrated. Symptoms of dehydration include fatigue, headache, and decreased coordination and judgment. When you are hiking, your body's rate of fluid loss depends on the outside temperature, humidity, altitude, and your activity level. On average, a hiker walking in warm weather will lose four liters of fluid a day. That fluid loss is easily replaced by normal consumption of liquids and food. However, if a hiker is walking briskly in hot, dry weather and hauling a heavy pack, he or she can lose one to three liters of water an hour. It's important to always carry plenty of water and to stop often and drink fluids regularly, even if you aren't thirsty.

Heat exhaustion is the result of a loss of large amounts of electrolytes and often occurs if a hiker is dehydrated and has been under heavy exertion. Common symptoms of heat exhaustion include cramping, exhaustion, fatigue, lightheadedness, and nausea. You can treat heat exhaustion by getting out of the sun and drinking an electrolyte solution made up of one teaspoon of salt and one tablespoon of sugar dissolved in a liter of water. Drink this solution slowly over a period of one hour. Drinking plenty of fluids (preferably an electrolyte solution/sports drink) can prevent heat exhaustion. Avoid hiking during the hottest parts of the day, and wear breathable clothing, a wide-brimmed hat, and sunglasses.

Hiking with Children

Hiking with children isn't a matter of how many miles you can cover or how much elevation gain you make in a day; it's about seeing and experiencing nature through their eyes.

Kids like to explore and have fun. They like to stop and point out bugs and plants, look under rocks, jump in puddles, and throw sticks. If you're taking a toddler or young child on a hike, start with a trail that you're familiar with. Trails that have interesting things for kids, like piles of leaves to play in or a small stream to wade through during the summer, will make the hike much more enjoyable for them and will keep them from getting bored.

You can keep your child's attention if you have a strategy before starting on the trail. Using games is not only an effective way to keep a child's attention, it's also a great way to teach him or her about nature. Play hide and seek, where your child is the mouse and you are the hawk. Quiz children on the names of plants and animals. If your children are old enough, let them carry their own daypack filled with snacks and water. So that you are sure to go at their pace and not yours, let them lead the way. Playing follow the leader works particularly well when you have a group of children. Have each child take a turn at being the leader.

From spring through fall, you'll want your kids to wear a wide-brimmed hat to keep their face, head, and ears protected from the hot sun. Also, make sure your children wear sunscreen at all times. Choose a brand without Paba—children have sensitive skin and may have an allergic reaction to sunscreen that contains Paba. If you are hiking with a child younger than six months, don't use sunscreen or insect repellent. Instead, be sure that their head, face, neck, and ears are protected from the sun with a wide-brimmed hat, and that all other skin exposed to the sun is protected with the appropriate clothing.

Remember that food is fun. Kids like snacks so it's important to bring a lot of munchies for the trail. Stopping often for snack breaks is a fun way to keep the trail interesting. Raisins, apples, granola bars, crackers and cheese, cereal, and trail mix all make great snacks. If your child is old enough to carry her own backpack, fill it with treats before you leave. If your kids don't like drinking water, you can bring boxes of fruit juice.

Day Hiker Checklist

- ❏ camera/film
- ❏ compass/GPS unit
- ❏ pedometer
- ❏ daypack
- ❏ first-aid kit
- ❏ food
- ❏ guidebook
- ❏ headlamp/flashlight with extra batteries and bulbs
- ❏ hat
- ❏ insect repellent
- ❏ knife/multipurpose tool
- ❏ map
- ❏ matches in waterproof container and fire starter
- ❏ fleece jacket
- ❏ rain gear
- ❏ sunglasses
- ❏ sunscreen
- ❏ swimsuit
- ❏ watch
- ❏ water
- ❏ water bottles/water hydration system

About the Author

Keith Stelter is a columnist for the HCN newspaper group and has been hiking, writing, and taking photographs for forty years. He has hiked national park trails with his father, and for the past six years, he has hiked extensively in the Houston, Austin–San Antonio areas. Keith served as executive director of the Texas Outdoor Writers Association in 2006 and 2007 and is a member of the Outdoor Writers Association of America, Texas Master Naturalists, North American Nature Photographers Association, and American Trails Association. He is the author of several books about Texas, including *Best Hikes Near Austin and San Antonio* and Best Easy Day Hikes guides to Austin and San Antonio. He lives in Tomball, Texas.

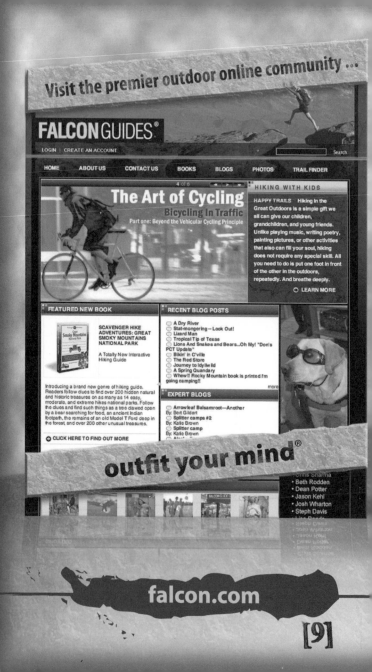